CHILD PLACEMENT:
PRINCIPLES AND PRACTICE

Second Edition

Child Placement: Principles and Practice

Second Edition

June Thoburn

arena

First published 1988 by Wildwood House Ltd

Second edition published by
Arena
Ashgate Publishing Limited
Gower House
Croft Road
Aldershot
Hants GU11 3HR
England

Ashgate Publishing Company
Old Post Road
Brookfield
Vermont 05036
USA

British Library Cataloguing in Publication Data

Thoburn, June
    Child Placement: Principles and Practice
    I. Title
    362.7

ISBN 1 85742 119 1

Typeset in 10pt Palatino by Bournemouth Colour Graphics,
Bournemouth, Dorset and printed in Great Britain by
Hartnolls Limited, Bodmin, Cornwall

Contents

List of check-lists

Acknowledgements

This book owes most to my former clients; to those on the receiving end of child placement services interviewed in the course of my research studies; and to the MA and Advanced Certificate students at the University of East Anglia and guardians *ad litem* who have contributed their own experiences to the courses on which it is based. My thanks to them all, and also to the many colleagues in social work teams and in the research teams working on the Department of Health-funded studies of child placement and child protection who have shared their ideas with me.

My thinking about child care was originally shaped by Olive Stevenson and Joan Warren, my tutor and my fieldwork supervisor at Barnett House, Oxford. Their wise and compassionate words have stood me in good stead over the years. All my colleagues in the School of Social Work at the University of East Anglia, especially Caroline Ball, Diana Hinings and David Howe, have helped me to make sense of changes in law and practice. I am grateful to them all, and especially to Martin Davies and Peter Wedge for their encouragement and constructive criticism. I acknowledge also the debt I owe to the many writers to whose work I refer, and especially to Greg Kelly who provided up-to-date information on child care statistics and law in Northern Ireland.

Anne Borrett and Grace Granger I thank for grappling with the word processor and my much amended manuscript. Finally thanks to John and Alan for putting up with the clutter and vagueness which seem to be the inevitable accompaniments of my writing endeavours.

For the end result, including any errors and omissions, I alone am responsible.

Introduction

This book, which was first published in 1988, is based on my own social work practice with children at risk and their families in Britain and Canada, and on my experience as a teacher of child care practice to social work students at qualifying and post-qualifying level. Its purpose is to offer practical guidance to those who have to take the difficult decisions about placing those vulnerable children looked after by the local authority, and then to put those decisions into effect in a way which is most conducive to improving the welfare of the children themselves, and those who are close to them. It concentrates on those who are at risk of remaining permanently separated from their families of origin in long-term care and is not, therefore, a general text on social work with children and their families. In particular it does not cover in detail the vitally important area of social work support to children in need living in their own homes, including children who have been abused or neglected but continue to live with their parents. It thus complements Jean Moore's *The ABC of Child Abuse Work* (1986) and *The ABC of Child Protection* (1992) also published by Arena. Nor does it treat in any detail the important dimensions of child care history (see especially Packman 1981, Holman 1988, and Parker 1990), or the political and social policy aspects (see especially Holman 1976, 1978, Jordan 1973, 1990, and Parton 1991). In this second edition changes have been made to incorporate new legislation, most notably the Children Act 1989 and the accompanying guidance.

The years between the passing of the Children Acts of 1975

and 1989 have seen many new developments in child care policy and practice. In the 1970s and early 1980s emphasis was placed on 'permanence policies' and the increased use of adoption for a wider range of children who could not return to their original families. Other important developments were the decreasing use of residential care and the spread of family centres (see especially Holman 1988, Gibbons *et al.* 1990, and Gibbons 1992). It is in the nature of things that new ideas must be implemented before they can be evaluated. The first edition of this book was written after the publication of the research reports summarised in the 1985 DHSS review *Social Work Decisions in Child Care* made it a particularly opportune time to incorporate British and American research findings in a text about the practice of child placement. This second edition incorporates research summarised in the 1991c DH publication *Patterns and Outcomes in Child Placement* as well as taking account of changes in practice resulting from the Children Act 1989.

The reader will find more references to research findings than might usually be expected in a practice handbook, since the main focus of the book is on decisions and practice at the time of placement. Such decisions must be informed by knowledge about which sort of placement and which model of practice is most likely to be effective for what sort of child in what circumstances. The approach taken is to view the contribution of knowledge in the terms outlined by England (1986, pp. 28–35) in his exploration of the characteristics of understanding, which he considers to be the basis of helping in social work. England notes that 'the worker's first task is to establish his own evaluation of the client's meaning; it is this "meaning" given by the client to his experience which shapes the nature of the problem and of the response of the worker'. After considering the importance of the use of self in understanding meaning, England writes that

> the role of the worker's 'defined' knowledge is to inform his understanding; he will understand more or understand quicker because of his professional learning – social workers can be prepared in general terms for situations which they will probably encounter, but they must be clear – and not apologetic – that such knowledge only serves to sketch in the likely characteristics of experience.

The Children Act 1989 required the court to make the child's welfare the paramount consideration but not to make an order 'unless it considers that doing so would be better for the child than making no order at all' (Section 1, 5). The worker preparing a report for the court thus has a duty to be familiar with whatever knowledge may be relevant to decisions about the impact and likely outcome of alternative placements and practice for each individual child. But knowledge will rarely be enough on its own. In my experience, an 'imaginative leap' is almost always needed to make the connection between knowledge and understanding – which is necessary for accurate empathy to be conveyed, and the appropriate decisions to be taken.

The other essential ingredients of effective practice are skill in communicating, especially with children to help them convey what their situation means to them; and skill in working with them to help bring about necessary change. It also requires the ability to provide support and care in those situations which cannot be significantly improved.

Finally reference must be made to the important question of the relationship between law and practice. In the belief that a little knowledge is worse than useless, I do not attempt to include a summary of child care law, and will assume that the reader has access to one of the texts on the Children Act 1989. In 1988 when the first edition was written I referred to 'the inconsistencies and complexity of present child care law'. We now have in England and Wales a comprehensive legal framework but it is still early days in understanding how the law will be translated into practice. In addition there are inconsistencies between adoption law and child care law. Possible changes in adoption law are discussed in the consultative document of the Department of Health and Welsh Office (1992).

In the chapters which follow, I offer a framework for practice, based on my own understanding of the knowledge available and on my own 'practice wisdom', and that of the colleagues and clients I have worked with, interviewed during my research or taught on a variety of qualifying and post-qualifying courses. It is of necessity selective, the decisions about what to include being based on my answer to the question, 'what do social workers need to know before they undertake child placement work, and what tips can I offer about effective practice?' The brief case examples are based on 'real' families with details and names

changed, and are intended to provide stimulus material to provoke group discussion or further thought, especially for those
who have not yet embarked on child care work. More experienced workers may prefer to ask themselves similar questions
with regard to children and families from their own case loads.

For them and for guardians *ad litem* the book should provide a
useful *aide-mémoire*, as well as helping them to introduce knowledge from new research into their practice. Time for reading is a
precious commodity, and the list of useful texts on social work
practice with children and families gets longer and longer. As
well as listing my sources in the bibliography I have therefore
included in Appendix 2 a very brief reading list of what I consider to be the most useful references about practice.

Finally a note about legal terminology. The new language of
the Children Act 1989 will be used wherever possible. Thus children who are being looked after by a local authority following a
court order are referred to as children in care, while those who
are being cared for at the request of parents or of the older children themselves are referred to as 'accommodated'. The term
'looked after' includes both groups. When referring to or quoting
from texts which pre-date the 1989 Act, however, the language
of 'in care' will often be used to include both groups.

1 Children looked after by local authorities and their families

Before starting to work with children needing placement away from home, it is essential to know as much as possible about them and their circumstances, and about the chances of success of the different placement options. Thanks to Department of Health research initiatives (DHSS 1985, DH 1991c), we now know a great deal about the children who are looked after by local authority social services departments and about their parents and those who care for them. Our knowledge of children living away from home in hospitals and boarding schools, as well as our knowledge about their parents and those who care for them, is more limited.

The researchers, who between them studied thousands of children considered for care in over 50 local authorities, tell us not only what happened to the children, but how social workers set about making decisions about them and how they, their parents and their social workers felt about the process. The newcomer to child care statistics should be alerted to the important distinction between statistics about children who *come into care* or are accommodated in any one year, and those which relate to children *actually being looked after* on 31 March in any one year (DH 1993). For the purposes of this book, which is principally concerned with those children at risk of remaining for long periods away from their families of origin, the 'looked after' figures (55 532 in England in 1992) are marginally more important since they include more of those who have been away from home for some time.

Contrary to the generally held view that children looked after by local authorities are young children rescued from inadequate or neglectful parents (a view encouraged by the media's concentration on child abuse), the majority of children (64 per cent in 1990 and 1991) are admitted at the request of, or with the consent of, their parents. (There was a move towards more compulsion, as indicated by the figure of 80 per cent of voluntary admissions in 1974, but the Children Act 1989 appears to have resulted in a swing back towards the accommodation of children on a voluntary basis. In the first six months after the implementation of the Act, 84 per cent of those entering care or accommodation did so voluntarily. Just under half of those admitted in 1990 were aged ten or over, and 9 per cent of the total were aged 16 or over when they left home. Thirty-five per cent were under five and only 6 per cent were aged between five and nine.)

Of the 55 000 or so children actually looked after in March 1992, only 17 per cent were under five, and 61 per cent were aged ten or over, with almost a quarter of the total population being aged 16 or over. Only a third of these children were 'accommodated', and 67 per cent were in care as a result of court orders.

The studies by Millham and his colleagues (1986, 1989) and Vernon and Fruin (1986) go some way towards explaining the differences in these two sets of statistics. In tracing 450 children who came into the care of five contrasting local authorities in 1980 for a period of two years, Millham *et al.* found that 62 per cent were no longer in care. One hundred and sixty-three (36 per cent of the whole group) had left care within six weeks, and those under five at admission were particularly likely to be discharged quickly. Thirty-four per cent of the children still in care were either home 'on trial' or fostered with relatives, leaving 110 of the original 450 children still in care and away from home at the two-year stage (24 per cent). Only 25 (15 per cent) of the 166 children who were aged five or under on admission to care, were still in care living away from home or relatives, compared with 34 per cent of the children who were aged between 6 and 11 on coming into care, and 31 per cent of those who came into care when they were aged 12 or over.

This profile of the children in long-term care is particularly important since it emphasises that it is children past infancy who are most at risk of remaining within the care system. This fact seems not to be sufficiently recognised in the child care policy statements issued by many local authorities.

In their concern to set time limits in order to avoid young children drifting in inappropriate placements, they may have been giving insufficient attention to the needs of older children, most of whom are likely to have some degree of attachment to their birth families, and who can therefore not be easily placed with permanent substitute families. Around 90 per cent of all children who are looked after by local authorities, as Millham and his colleagues make clear, will eventually return to their natural families, or at least to live independently in the same neighbourhoods, in some cases after being looked after away from home for several years.

The families of children looked after by local authorities

As well as giving a picture of the ages, placement and legal status of children coming into care, the recent studies also describe their family circumstances. In most respects the picture emerging is similar to that of studies of children in care in the 1950s and 1960s, except that fewer children, thanks in no small part to the practical help provisions of Section 1 of the Children and Young Persons Act 1963 (repeated again in the Child Care Act 1980) and the Housing (Homeless Persons) Act 1977, now come into care for purely practical reasons such as homelessness or confinement or short-term physical illness of a parent. However, recent administrative policies, necessitated by the growth of homelessness and lack of affordable housing stock, have tightened up on criteria for acceptance as homeless. In particular more families are now deemed to have made themselves 'intentionally homeless'. Whilst homelessness alone is still not considered a valid reason for the provision of local authority accommodation, there is no doubt that stress resulting from housing problems is increasingly a contributory factor to family breakdown and the need for accommodation for children.

Deprivation
All the recent studies show that children looked after by local

authorities come disproportionately from working-class families, or from families where the only source of income is state benefit. Despite the increase in home ownership in recent years, the families involved are more likely to live in rented accommodation, especially council accommodation. Packman and her colleagues (1986) found that one in five of the children considered for care lived in 'poor, run-down inner city areas' (p. 36). Bebbington and Miles (1989) found that the chances of needing local authority accommodation increased from one in 7000 to one in ten if a child aged between five and nine was in a household dependent on income support; had a single parent; had three or more siblings; was of mixed ethnic origin; and lived in private rented accommodation where there were one or more person per room.

The relationship between material disadvantage and reception into care is complex and has been explored at length in the 'cycle of disadvantage' studies (see especially Essen and Wedge 1982, Fuller and Stevenson 1983, Madge 1983, and Blackburn 1991). Although children from disadvantaged families *are* overrepresented, not *all* those who are looked after are materially disadvantaged, and the majority of children in disadvantaged families remain at home. Millham and his colleagues (1986) note that the primary reasons for admission to care were breakdown in family care (in 69 per cent of cases) and the behaviour of the child (in 25 per cent of cases). The case histories in Millham *et al.* and Packman *et al.* give ample support for the views expressed by Jordan (1973), Holman (1976) and Parton (1981) that the stresses placed on families by adverse living conditions contribute to the breakdown of family relationships which itself makes children particularly vulnerable to coming into care or accommodation. Thus whilst the numbers actually looked after because of homelessness are few, the stresses placed on families who are accommodated in bed and breakfast hotels may lead to marital discord or psychiatric disturbance, which precipitate a request for accommodation or a child protection investigation. In a recent study of 220 consecutive cases referred to seven local authorities because of child protection concerns, families in council or private rented accommodation and those entirely dependent on income support were greatly overrepresented. In only 36 per cent of cases was income received from regular employment, and only 17 per cent of the parents were owner-occupiers

(Thoburn and Lewis 1992).

Rowe and her colleagues, comparing their sample of 200 children who had been in the care of five different local authorities for at least four years (including some teenagers who had been in care all their lives), with a sample of 200 children placed recently in foster care by the same authorities, found that the later-placed group had come into care when they were significantly older and were more likely to have been admitted because of a temporary crisis or because of abuse, neglect or rejection. Recently placed children were more likely to have behaviour difficulties, and their parents were described as 'a group of parents with very severe problems indeed. Not only were they facing practical difficulties which would daunt the most capable individual, but in so many cases they have major personal problems as well.' (Rowe *et al.* 1984: 215). The studies described in the Department of Health (1991c) review of research (see especially Bebbington and Miles 1989, and Rowe *et al.* 1989) indicate that this trend has continued.

Changing families

The most striking feature of the families of children who are looked after is the transient nature of family relationships. Children from single parent families have always been at greater risk of coming into care, but the higher incidence of marital breakdown, combined with a tendency to remarry, has led to a higher incidence of children from 'changing' or 'reconstituted' families coming into care (see particularly Lambert and Streather 1980, and Burgoyne and Clark 1982). One in five of the 361 children considered for care in Packman and her colleagues' (1986) sample were living with step-parents and only half of the children who were living with siblings lived with only 'natural' brothers and sisters. The rest shared their parents with step-, half- or adopted brothers and sisters. Forty per cent of the children were living in single parent families and 56 per cent had lived through marital breakdown.

Millham *et al.* (1986) found that children were particularly likely to come into care following a crisis, or difficult behaviour on the part of the child, when the family was in the process of 'reconstituting'. Forty-five per cent of the children studied by Millham and his colleagues came into care from single parent families, and in only 27 per cent of cases were the children living with both natural parents. Not only did the children have to cope with change, but the change was often precipitate, and accompanied by violence. Farmer and Parker (1991) found that 31 per cent of 172 children who were in care for reasons of protection returned home to a parent and new partner, and 16 per cent returned to a different parent or relative from the one with whom they had their home when they went into care. They noted particular difficulties for those who returned to a family with a new step-sibling who was born whilst they were in care.

As well as experiencing change *within* their families, a high proportion of the children had been cared for outside their family home, either by relatives or because of previous admissions into care. Rowe and her colleagues (1984) note that 70 per cent of the children who had been in care for at least five years were admitted before their second birthday, compared with only 40 per cent of the more recently placed children. They also note, however, that at least 60 per cent of those placed more recently had been cared for away from their parents at least once prior to the recent admission to care. In the course of these various moves, many parents, especially natural fathers, become lost to the children. Social workers did not know of the whereabouts of the natural fathers of a third of the children studied by Millham and his colleagues. Not surprisingly, in view of this pattern of movement, families of children looked after by local authorities are often estranged from their extended families.

As this book is being revised the Child Support Act 1991 is being implemented. It remains to be seen whether this will help to keep more children in touch with absent parents and their relatives, or whether, as some commentators fear, it will exacerbate tensions between separated parents and make contact for the children more difficult. The new provisions in the Children Act 1989 which are designed to help both parents to continue to exercise parental responsibility after separation have not yet been evaluated.

Health and disability

Although health problems of the parents are less frequently cited as reasons for care or accommodation than used to be the case, the studies show that they are a significant cause of stress. Social workers interviewed by Packman considered that 30 per cent of the mothers suffered from some form of mental disorder, ranging from mild anxiety to acute and chronic mental illness. The workers considered that one in ten mothers was in poor physical health, and even more of the families interviewed considered that poor physical health had significantly added to the stresses in the families. Berridge and Cleaver (1987) found that 17 per cent of the parents of 189 children in long-term care had mental health problems at the time the child left home. In 1990 over 4 000 children (14 per cent) entered care mainly because of the illness of a parent or guardian, but this ignores the number of cases where illness was a contributory factor. The growing incidence of AIDS amongst parents should be noted and some agencies are giving careful consideration to the special needs of their children (Batty 1993).

The Children Act 1989 places services for children who have disabilities firmly within the legal context of service for all children. Accurate figures for the number of children who have disabilities and who are cared for by local authorities for short or long periods are not yet available. This is because many respite schemes operated informally outside child care legislation prior to 1991. Also many children with disabilities are cared for away from home in health service establishments. It has become increasingly clear in recent years that children who have disabilities are even more vulnerable to a range of adversities, from losing a parent through marital breakdown to being abused by strangers or carers. The work of the 'Keep deaf children safe' project has illustrated this with one group of children with disabilities, and a volume of *Child Abuse Review* was devoted to the subject (Kennedy and Kelly 1992).

Black children and those from other minority ethnic groups

Finally in this brief review of the family circumstances of children looked after by local authorities, mention must be made of the position of black children and those from other minority ethnic groups.

The Children Act 1989 (Schedule 2, para. 1) required local authorities to 'have regard to the different racial groups to which children within their area who are in need belong' and to ensure that the cultural needs of children from different ethnic groups are met when they are looked after. This should ensure that information about the ethnicity of children receiving services will in future be more systematically collected. At the moment it is difficult to be sure whether black children are, as some commentators believe, more likely to be in care or accommodated by local authorities (Ahmed *et al.* 1986). The most systematic study is that of Rowe and her colleagues (1989). In that study, 19 per cent of children admitted to care between 1985 and 1987 were from minority ethnic groups. There were, however, big differences in admission rates between ethnic minority groups, and also differences between their careers in care. Children whose parents were both Asian were underrepresented, whilst children whose parents were both African or Carribean were more likely than other groups to come into care, but their stay in care was likely to be as a result of voluntary arrangements and of short duration. However, black children of mixed parentage were far more likely than white children or children whose parents were both black to come into care in the first place, and to remain longer in care. This tendency was even more marked in areas where black people account for only a small proportion of the population. This question of black children is discussed fully in the Department of Health review of research which accompanied the 1989 Act (DH 1991) and the implications of the Act for black children and families are very helpfully explored in a publication of the Race Equality Unit (Macdonald 1991).

Children looked after for extended periods

If we now turn to consider those children who remain away from home for longer periods, the characteristics noted amongst those who experience periods of being looked after by the local authority become even more marked. Millham and his colleagues noted that the composition of the children's families continued to undergo change after they came into care.

The natural families of nearly three-quarters (73 per cent) of those

admitted to care before the age of eleven had changed radically during the child's absence as compared with just half (54 per cent) for
the older age groups. Children on care orders for neglect or because
of moral danger display much higher rates of family change (85 per
cent) than do those in other legislative categories such as those in
voluntary care (55 per cent), care orders for being beyond control or
in need of full-time education (48 per cent), delinquency (53 per cent)
and cases where full parental rights have been assumed (54 per cent).
(Millham *et al.* 1986: 194)

By the two-year stage, only 29 per cent of the natural parents
were still living together compared with 41 per cent at the time
of admission to care. This is accounted for by the fact that children from two parent families were more likely to leave care
more quickly, as well as by disintegrating relationships whilst
the child was in care.

It has already been noted that black children of mixed parentage also tend to stay longer in care.

In contrast, children with severe physical or learning disabilities do not figure highly in the statistics, but it has already been
noted that this may give a false picture because until recently if
they were unable to be cared for by their natural families, they
tended to remain in long-stay hospitals.

The children and their difficulties

Packman and her colleagues (1986) divided the children who
may come into care into three groups: the 'victims', the 'volunteereds' and the 'villains'. Vernon and Fruin (1986) found that
the children they studied fell into similar categories. However,
both found considerable overlap between the three groups, especially in the eyes of the parents. Although the 'villains' were the
group defined by social workers as needing care because of their
own actions or problems, such as not going to school or commit-
ting offences, all the researchers show that problem behaviour in
the children who were categorised either as 'victims' or 'volunteereds' was often a contributory factor. Fisher and his colleagues (1986) show how the inability of youngsters to adjust to
family changes, divided loyalties and new patterns of control
when families reconstituted, could increase family stress to such
an extent that parents asked for their children to be looked after
by local authorities. Packman showed how many of the parents

whose children were eventually committed to care had previously requested accommodation as a means of providing help for children whose behaviour was difficult. The emphasis for the 'volunteered' and the 'victims' tends to be on the behaviour of the parents, in no small part because as the law then stood, problems displayed by the children were not grounds either for voluntary reception into care, or for statutory action, other than for children who were beyond control. Although, therefore, in the currently available statistics there is no category for younger children who come into care because of their own difficulties, such as severe physical or learning disabilities, many in fact do so under the 'unsatisfactory home conditions' or 'other reasons' categories.

Statistics collected following the Children Act 1989 should give a clearer picture. It will be particularly interesting to note any changes resulting from the fact that young persons aged 16 or 17 may themselves ask for accommodation, and may decide to remain in accommodation irrespective of the wishes of their parents.

It is not therefore surprising to find that many of the children in care described by the researchers did have serious problems. Rowe and her colleagues (1984) found that 44 per cent of the recently placed children had at least one major – or two minor – behaviour problems at the time of placement in their foster homes. Problems included: eating problems, temper tantrums, difficulty in making relationships, stealing, lying and difficulty in concentrating. Packman and colleagues (1986) found that 4 per cent of the 'volunteered' children and 10 per cent of the 'victims', as well as 73 per cent of the 'villains', were delinquent; that 7 per cent of the 'volunteered' and 16 per cent of the 'victims', as well as 42 per cent of the 'villains', were truants; and that 30 per cent of the 'volunteered' children and 13 per cent of the 'victims', were described as 'unmanageable'. '"Villains", "victims" and "volunteereds" were *not* clearly demarcated groups, but occupied different but overlapping places along a spectrum, or family life span, of deprivation and disruption' (Packman *et al.* 1986: 62–63). Fisher *et al.* (1986) note that difficulties over the care of 350 children all aged over eight were extremely long-standing. In a recent study of 1 152 children in care referred for permanent family placement, Thoburn and Rowe (in Fratter *et al.* 1991) found that 29 per cent were described as 'institutionalised', 50 per cent were reported to have behaviour difficulties and 63 per cent to have emotional problems. Whilst some of these children had been in care for many years, and their behaviour difficulties had been compounded by moves within care, others had been away from their parents for comparatively brief periods of time. If anything, these figures understate the problems of the children themselves, since children in temporary placements are, to an extent, in 'cold storage'. Their problems often only show up in the context of close relationships so that they may appear relatively 'problem free' until they are again required to form close attachments to natural or substitute parents. Increasingly children who were not previously known to have been abused have started to tell their carers about earlier abusive experiences, which almost invariably have an impact on their behaviour. Macaskill (1991) and Batty (1991) have produced helpful guides for carers of children who have been sexually abused.

To conclude, this review of the characteristics of children looked after by local authorities and of their parents has shown a formidable array of difficulties which must be faced by caregivers, children and social workers if subsequent placements are to be successful. Perhaps even more importantly planners and managers need to be aware of the characteristics and histories of the children to be placed, if placement and other resources are to match the needs of the children in their care.

2 A review of social work practice in child placement

Family support services

The research studies are all agreed that social work before family breakdown, and when children leave home, has considerable impact on their experiences of being looked after and the long-term impact of this experience. Although all the writers so far mentioned argue that voluntary care (accommodation) should be – in the spirit of all post-war legislation – an integral part of preventive social work service, they found that this was rarely the case in practice. The move towards more children coming into care statutorily throughout the 1970s and 1980s has already been noted. Despite the many articles in the professional literature about services to families whose children may be at risk (most usually involving family centres, or family therapy teams), the researchers did *not* find that the majority of the children came into care only after well-planned services to the families in their own homes had proved ineffective. Packman and her colleagues (1986) found that if care was refused, little positive help was offered instead, and although many of the families were 'well known' to the social services department before the care episode, this did not usually mean that they were being offered appropriate help. The cumulative weight of this research led to the strong emphasis in the Children Act 1989 on the provision of a range of support services to children in need and their families in their own homes.

Fisher and his colleagues (1986) described social workers fighting a rearguard action to prevent the children coming into care, while parents kept up the pressure to achieve placement in care which *they* considered an appropriate means of helping their children and themselves. They saw the social workers' ability to be helpful as being severely limited by their inability to understand their points of view as parents.

Apart from Mattinson and Sinclair's (1979) report of their action research on the feasibility of undertaking marital social work within a social services department, and one or two small studies appearing in the journals (mainly of in-house work with a behavioural or family therapy focus), there were no British empirical studies of social work in the 1980s which aimed to keep children out of care. The position in America is somewhat different. In pursuing permanency policies many states have set up specialist projects which aim to ensure permanence for children at risk by supporting them with their natural families or helping them to return to them – in the same way that permanence units in Britain have been set up to find *substitute* families for children in care.

The most important American studies are those by Mary Ann Jones and her colleagues (1976, 1985) which evaluate a range of preventive and rehabilitative services to families. These studies conclude that intensive services are more successful at keeping children out of care and returning them from care than the usual services on offer. They also indicate that, within specialist services, those which last longer and involve a range of practical and casework services are more successful than higher intensity but shorter duration services using psychodynamic or behavioural methods to achieve change. These conclusions about the style of social work most likely to be effective in supporting children in their own homes are similar to those of Maluccio and his colleagues (1986), also in America, and Packman and her colleagues (1986) and Fisher and his colleagues (1986) in Britain. More recently accounts have been appearing of the evaluation of 'family preservation services' which similarly use a combination of practical help and emotional support, but of an even higher intensity over a very short period (Whittaker *et al.* 1990). Apart from the very short time-scale, the work is very similar to the intensive family work of Family Service Units in Britain in the

1970s. Drawing on their research findings, all these authors stress the importance of a participatory model of work involving a combination of practical help (including where necessary respite care or a 'shared care' model of accommodation), and therapeutic endeavour which has the agreement and participation of family members.

Coming into care or accommodation

The effect of such services not being available – and often being frowned upon as an inappropriate response to stress within families – was that, as the researchers found, many children, including those well known to social workers, came into care in emergencies. A third of those studied by Millham *et al.* (1986) and by Packman *et al.* (1986), including many older children whom the researchers did not consider to be at risk, came into care on place of safety orders. In the case of many of the others, social workers suddenly 'caved in' to pressure – sometimes from other agencies but sometimes from the parents themselves – and made emergency placements.

Not surprisingly, therefore, admissions were badly managed, with little or no time to choose an appropriate placement or prepare children, parents and care-givers for the admission. A further result was that many of the initial placements were unsatisfactory. Millham and his colleagues (1986) found that 136 of the 222 children still in care at six months had changed their placements, and that two-thirds of the 48 placements which broke down in the first six months did so in crisis conditions necessitating a hasty move. Once again the child was unprepared for a move, almost certainly to an inappropriate placement which again was therefore unlikely to last. Berridge and Cleaver (1987, p. 74) show that 21 and 42 per cent of children fostered long-term with strangers by two local authorities experienced placement breakdown within three years, and that many long-term placements were made in a hurry following a previous breakdown. A fifth of the children 'had packed their toys and toothbrushes within a week, and another 9 per cent did so within a fortnight'. Unsurprisingly these placements were particularly unsettled, with breakdown rates of 50 per cent. By the two-year stage, 67 of the 170 children still in care studied by Millham *et al.* had experienced placement breakdowns, in 55 cases necessitating a hasty transfer. The 170 children had experienced 505 different placements.

This study, and that of Berridge and Cleaver (1987), showed that children in voluntary care experienced fewer breakdowns of placement than those in statutory care. These, and their own findings, encourage Packman *et al.* to restate their belief that

> when choices are to be made, ... voluntary care should be the preferred mode of entry and not, as it appears at present, a course to be taken reluctantly or apologetically. There is clear evidence that the admission process and the care experience itself are likely to be less distressing for the child or young person and certainly less upsetting for his parents. (Packman *et al.* 1986: 200)

They further suggest that instead of seeing admission to care as a last resort, policy statements should give 'detailed guidance as to what kinds of admission are best avoided and how prevention might be achieved, and suggestions about which admissions may actually be beneficial, and why' (p. 197). Packman and her colleagues conclude that the attitude which sees reception into care as something to be avoided becomes a self-fulfilling prophesy in that precipitate and unplanned entries into care caused by this 'goal-keeping' policy help to ensure that in many cases care is indeed a distressing and harmful experience.

> A 'rule of pessimism' operated about the care system, which meant that admission was sometimes almost unthinkable, until it became too late to think at all. 'Last resorts' are, after all, seldom desirable or constructive places to be. (Packman *et al.* 1986: 197)

The studies also show that, despite extensive evidence about the value of continued parental contact for the majority of children, social workers and systems erect unnecessary barriers to contact and that links between children in care and members of their birth families quickly wither away. (See especially Millham *et al.* 1986. I return to this important subject in Chapter 3.) These studies had a significant impact on the Children Act 1989, which stresses the fundamental importance of working in partnership with parents, relatives and older children, and places the provision of accommodation for children alongside day care and other services as an essential element of support rather than something to be avoided. Prevention is no longer equated with preventing children from coming into care, but rather with preventing long-term family breakdown and the abuse of children in their own homes or away from home.

Management issues

All the studies note the influence of management policies on practice, and the increased tendency for decisions to be taken by panels or committees from which the families and children are often excluded. We return to this point in Chapter 3 but note here that Marsh concludes from the research studies that this increasing bureaucratisation of planning may in part explain the increase in emergency admissions and their adverse consequences.

> The extent and complexity of discussions seemed at times to be excessive, and there appeared to be a number of occasions when the type of procedure had a greater effect on outcome than the preference of the client or the worker. If it is easy to obtain an emergency place, and cumbersome to obtain a planned one, it is likely that emergencies will occur more often. (Marsh 1986: 24)

Volumes 2 and 3 of the Children Act 1989, *Regulations and Guidance*, and *Working Together under the Children Act 1989* (DH 1991b), on cases of alleged child maltreatment, stress the importance of involving parents and children at planning meetings and reviews.

Placement with substitute families

If the message from research is that the management of the initial move from home and the early months in care leaves much to be desired for a substantial proportion of children, research findings on the placement with substitute families of children who cannot return home is more encouraging. Reviews of the placement of 'special needs' children with permanent substitute families by specialist agencies (Wedge and Thoburn 1986, and Thoburn 1990), show breakdown rates within two years ranging from 5 to 22 per cent, with the risks of breakdown being greater if the child is older when placed. The studies show that such placements for young children who have physical or learning disabilities are almost unproblematic, whereas those for older youngsters – especially if they are behaviourally or emotionally disturbed – are more risky and need considerable post-placement support. Sadly, though, there are indications that children who have a history of abuse and deprivation are more likely to experience placement breakdown than those who have not (Fratter *et al.* 1991).

American studies involving larger numbers in placement for longer periods give a similar picture. (See especially Stein *et al.* 1978, Lahti 1982, Fein *et al.* 1983, and Nelson 1985.) Unlike their British counterparts, American permanent placement units have 'return home' as the first option, and have had considerable success in achieving permanence by this route for children who had been assessed as unlikely to return home.

I shall discuss these studies in more detail when I come to consider the different placement options, but turn now to the implications which old and new knowledge have for child placement practice.

3 Principles for practice

A study of the consumer literature and the research reports leads me to the following principles for effective child care social work practice, whatever the placement. A comprehensive discussion of the principles which should inform good child care practice is to be found in the DH (1989b) publication which accompanied the Children Act, *The Care of Children: Principles and Practices in Regulations and Guidance*. It is essential in my view that anyone working in child and family social work has their own copy of this booklet and regularly refers to it when evaluating their own practice, or confronting dilemmas and choices.

I have found it helpful to organise my thinking about practice around three different but overlapping frameworks built up during my initial training and modified as further evidence has come to light with practice experience and new research findings. First the parameters for work are set by professional and personal values, and by legal requirements and constraints. Second we all develop over time 'frameworks for understanding', based on the social science disciplines and especially on what we know about human growth and behaviour and about how individuals function in society. Our understanding is also informed by what we learn from our clients as we work to understand the meaning which they place on the various events in their lives. Third we need frameworks which enable us to work with clients and colleagues in putting together 'helping packages' for different sorts of people, at different stages in their lives.

The legal and professional framework

Who is the client?

The first principle underlying decisions about the placement of children and methods of working with them and their families, is that first priority must be given in the short-term to protecting them from serious physical or emotional harm, and, in the long-term, to promoting their welfare throughout childhood and into adult life. It is sometimes assumed that the concept of promoting a child's welfare is unproblematic. In reality there can be considerable disagreement about how this may be achieved.

In training guardians *ad litem* for their role as independent advocates for children we start by asking them to read Fox-Harding's (1991) book on the value positions adopted by those working with children. While most fall somewhere between the two polarised positions of 'kinship defenders' and 'society as parent protagonists', it is essential for child care workers to identify their own values and be aware of their impact on individual decisions. In a study of social work with children who went home 'on trial' (Thoburn 1980), I found that while all the workers interviewed stated that they always gave first consideration to the welfare of the child, the amount of time which they were willing to spend on working with natural families could be related to the extent to which they considered that birth ties were important. We ask guardians *ad litem* to consider the case of Jenny outlined in Chapter 4 (see pages 70–72) and to decide which of the alternative placements would be most likely to promote her welfare. We have never as yet undertaken this exercise without finding the group split and someone able to put together coherent arguments in favour of each of the placement options. Although this is an artificial exercise – and more information would be available in an actual case which might point in one direction or another – it is a salutary reminder that there can be different views about the welfare of a child and that those views are likely to be influenced by the values held by those making the decisions.

The paramountcy of the child's welfare does *not* mean that the welfare of the adults concerned, especially parents, is unimportant. I dislike the widely used phrase 'the child is the prime client' (see, for example, the Beckford Report, London Borough of Brent 1985) since in my mind the concept of a prime client implies a secondary client, which can too easily be rationalised as sanctioning a second-rate or half-hearted service to the parents. Because looking after children away from home is so often seen as an admission of failure, parents who ask for their children to be accommodated or whose children come into care tend to be seen – and to see themselves – as failed parents. We know from research studies, and from the words of parents themselves, that the service they often receive falls far short of that implied by the British Association of Social Workers' (BASW) Code of Ethics, and by the document *Clients are Fellow Citizens* (BASW 1980). I have often heard that when workers discuss with managers their dilemmas about working with parents who have injured their children, they are asked to remember that their client is the child, as if their dilemma will then immediately disappear,

The *Principles and Practice* guide gives no such apparently easy way out:

> Parents are individuals with needs of their own. Even though services may be offered primarily on behalf of their children, parents are entitled to help and consideration in their own right. ....
>
> The development of a working partnership with parents is usually the most effective route to providing supplementary or substitute care for children. Measures which antagonise, alienate, undermine or marginalise parents are counter-productive. (DH 1989b: 8)

If the worker for the child is unable to gain the trust of the parents and offer them a service appropriate to their own needs, a second worker should be allocated. Clearly a part of that service will be to honestly help them understand that if there *is* conflict, decisions about the child's welfare will take precedence over their own needs and wishes. The offering of a first-class service to parents and close relatives of youngsters living away from home is important since, even if they are not to return home, the wellbeing of the parents continues to have an impact on the children's lives. We know that youngsters tend to take upon themselves a sense of responsibility for what happens to their parents. We also know that children's wellbeing is usually higher if satisfactory contact can be maintained (Thoburn 1990, and Fratter *et al.* 1991), and that this is more likely to happen if parents feel valued as people.

Thus services designed to improve the wellbeing of parents of children who are looked after by the local authority are not only necessary for ethical reasons – which stress 'the recognition of the value and dignity of every human being, irrespective of origin, status, sex, sexual orientation, age, belief, or contribution to society' (BASW Code of Ethics) – but also because increased parental wellbeing is likely to be in the interests of children.

Services to parents are also required by the Children Act 1989, and by statutory regulations, such as the Adoption Agencies' Regulations and the Children Act 1989 Guidance and Regulations. Section 17, 3, of the Act states that:

> Any service provided by an authority may be provided for the family of a particular child in need or for any member of his family, if it is provided with a view to safeguarding or promoting the child's welfare.

Even when children and parents do not have a future together, there is a clear duty to provide a service to parents. The Adoption Agencies' regulations (1983) are specific on this point, requiring the agency to provide a counselling service to the parents; and to explain and provide written information about procedures for adoption and about alternatives to adoption. The consultation document on proposed changes to adoption law suggests that parents should be offered a different social worker from that of their child to help them to take part more effectively in the planning and court process and to work out how they can continue to play a positive part in their children's future lives (DH 1992). The possibility of a Section 8 contact order being attached to an adoption order, though unlikely to be used often, reinforces the importance of the original parents to children even after adoption.

A partnership model of service

Ethical considerations, research about effectiveness, and the legal framework all point towards a model of social work service based on partnership – with natural parents and close relatives, with care-givers and with the children themselves whose rights to consultation are embodied in the requirement that:

> before making any decision with respect to a child whom they are looking after, or proposing to look after, a local authority shall, so far as is reasonably practicable, ascertain the wishes and feelings of a) the child; b) his parents; c) any person who has parental responsibility for him. (Section 22, 4)

Nor is it enough just to seek opinions. Having done so, the local authority must give due consideration to the opinions of parents, children and any other person whose wishes and feelings appear to be relevant.

Fisher and his colleagues (Fisher *et al.* 1986) and Marsh (1986) have indicated that often, despite the rhetoric of contracts and agreements, negotiations between social workers, parents whose children may come into care and the children themselves are distinctly one-sided. A partnership model of social work suggests the use of the supportive services of Part 3 of the Children Act wherever possible, and, if statutory powers have to be used, that the issue of power be honestly confronted. It will be very rare for a child found to be 'in need of protection' following a Section 47 investigation not to be a 'child in need' under Section 17. If the child can be adequately protected by working in partnership with family members under the provisions of Section 17, this is required by the 'no order' principle as well as being likely to be a more effective way of securing his or her long-term welfare.

While carers and parents of children in care have very little formal power when compared with that of social workers and courts, they may have considerable *informal* power – to visit or not to visit, to encourage or not to encourage parental visits, to work with social work plans or to obstruct them. They are more likely to use this power obstructively if they see the exercise of social-work power as unreasonable or incomprehensible. Fisher and his colleagues and Packman and her colleagues (1986) in Britain, and Maluccio *et al.* (1986, using an ecological model), and Stein *et al.* (1978, using a behavioural model) all advocate an 'empowerment' approach and give evidence of its effectiveness. Rees (1991) provides a critical analysis of issues of power in social work, and the Family Rights Group (1991) have produced a training pack and reader to help social workers to incorporate the partnership principles of the Children Act into their practice. Lewis *et al.* (1992), Marsh and Fisher (1992) and Thoburn (1992b) offer similar guidance in respect of child protection work.

Such an approach involves workers devolving as much of their power as possible to parents, children and care-givers. The sharing of knowledge is an important step towards empowerment. Shemmings (1991) stresses the importance of encouraging parents and children to take part in the writing of records as well as encouraging them to ask to see what is written about them.

Much has been written about the importance and the role of reviews (Parker 1980, McDonnell and Aldgate 1984, Sinclair 1984, Thoburn 1986, Vernon and Fruin 1986, Bryer 1988, and the British Agencies for Adoption and Fostering (BAAF) 1991). While the statutory reviews are an important fail-safe mechanism to ensure that work is being carried out appropriately, they can be no replacement for day-to-day work carried on in an atmosphere of partnership, trust and openness. The use of written agreements, and recording along the lines first outlined by Øvretveit (1986) and applied to children in the guidance to the Act, greatly increases the likelihood of successfully working together, although it does not guarantee it if workers do not genuinely believe in the desirability of sharing as much power as possible with their clients.

One reason why it might be difficult to achieve a partnership style of working is that departmental guidelines may be too rigid to allow for decisions to be tailored to individual cases. Although it is important to have *general* policy statements, based on research and political decisions about the best use of resources, it is essential that decisions are made for *each* child as an individual, if necessary involving the provision of a resource or service which runs contrary to what is generally available. Agencies which require social workers to follow blanket policies may find cases being taken to judicial review on the grounds that they are unlawfully fettering discretion.

A framework for understanding

Most theories of human growth, development and socialisation have something to offer to our understanding of children who may be accommodated or in care and of their care-givers, since environment and early relationships will have impinged on different individuals in different ways. While we all tend to incline towards one set of theories of personality development rather than another, it is important to keep an open mind in approaching each new situation in order to make the best use of the knowledge available to us. Maximé (in Ahmed *et al.* 1986) shows how social learning theory, object relations theory, and structural theories have all contributed to her understanding of the black children referred to her. Lowe (1987) finds cognitive theories, as well as psychoanalytic theories and organisation theory, help her to make sense of the anger of parents of children in care. In the field of child abuse Finkelhor *et al.* (1986) show how a range of theories can help us to understand the differential impact of different forms of abuse both in the short- and the long-term.

The topic is vast, but among the many general texts those I have found most helpful have been those of Bee (1989) and of Ford (1983) and, from a structural perspective, Leonard (1984). Rapoport and his colleagues (1982) describe the changing nature of the family in Britain, and Fahlberg's (1988) or Sheridan's (BAAF 1986) summaries of developmental milestones should be kept where they can be referred to easily. The *Assessment and Action Records* developed by Parker and his colleagues (1991) for reviewing the progress of children build on this body of knowledge.

Within the many theories that contribute to our understanding of children in care and their care-givers, however, I attach particular importance to those that discuss the development of a sense of identity (especially the work of Erikson 1965, 1983); and the impact of attachment, separation and loss on the lives of children and those who care for them (especially the work of Winnicott 1965, and Bowlby 1971, 1979, 1988). There are many useful summaries of this work now available (see especially Jewett 1984, and Fahlberg 1988).

A framework for helping

This framework for helping is based on a belief that, despite the many inadequacies pointed out in research reports and consumer studies, there are many children and families who have greatly benefitted from social work help, including placement in care. Fisher and his colleagues (1986) identified 25 per cent of families who found the social work service helpful and appropriate. The parents of children who had been in care, and the new 'permanent' parents and children themselves whom I have interviewed in the course of my research (Thoburn 1980, Thoburn *et al.* 1986, and Thoburn 1990) had many positive things to say about some social workers. These positive comments, together with the comments of those young people who consider themselves to have been greatly helped by field and residential workers which alternate with less favourable remarks in the 'Who Cares?' literature, need to be set alongside negative consumer comments and adverse reports which hit the headlines.

Any framework for helping must include *knowledge* from research and practice wisdom about the effectiveness of different types of service in different circumstances to aid workers in their 'social care planning' roles; and familiarity with a range of social work *theories* and *skills*, which will be added to throughout their careers.

We all have our favourite ways of conceptualising the services we offer. I find it helpful to think simply in terms of relationships; deeds and services; and words or therapy. I also find a 'check-list' approach helpful (see check-lists 1, 2 and 3 in this chapter). Obviously the questions need to be answered with respect to the different people who may need a service and the answers will be different in each case, and at different times. Sometimes it will be appropriate to work with all those involved as a network, perhaps encompassing the care-givers as well as the natural family and child, or as a family group, or in a series of sub-groups. There is an ever-expanding literature on family therapy. More recently some agencies have adapted the New Zealand family group conference to the British situation (Ryburn 1992). Even when working with individuals, it is essential to use an approach which bears in mind the significance of the family, the network and the environment. Most often both family group-work *and* work with individuals will be appropriate. The nature of the service to be offered will also differ depending on the nature of the placement, and the stage that the placement has reached, and I shall return to this in the following chapters.

Relationships

The reason why we aim for 'permanence' for children in care is that it allows a youngster the opportunity to love and be loved for the foreseeable future. Care-givers and original parents have the same need to experience loving and lasting relationships. In assessing the nature of the professional helping relationship, therefore, the worker must consider the other relationships within the family, including the extended family, and the neighbourhood.

The advantage of the family therapy or family groupwork approach is that it emphasises and seeks to build on existing relationships, so that family members can meet each other's needs for love and support. However, for many families who are close to breaking point, family members are so caught up with practical, personal or relationship difficulties that they are

Check-list 1. Relationships

For whom?	With whom?
(step) mother	members of the family
(step) father	friends
non-resident parents	neighbours
each child	others in a similar situation
carer(s)	volunteer
carers' children	home care worker/family aide
	child's social worker
	another field or residential social worker (from own or another agency)
	group worker or group members (e.g. parent's aid groups, adopters or foster parent group, 'Who Cares' group, women's or men's group, 'handling' group, social skills group)
	other professional (e.g. teacher, health visitor, day care worker, GP, psychologist, psychiatrist, play therapist, youth or community worker, welfare rights or law centre worker)

unable to meet each other's needs without help. Thus the question frequently arises about what additional supportive and caring relationships can be offered. More often than not, these needs will be met by 'second-hand social work' – the social worker will encourage friends, neighbours and relatives as well as family members to provide emotional support to a parent or a youngster. Increasingly volunteers are being recruited to support families and youngsters through 'link-up' schemes for adolescents, or programmes which link parents with volunteer befrienders such as Home-start (Van der Eyken 1982) or NEWPIN (Cox *et al.* 1992). Gibbons *et al.* (1990) and Gibbons (1992) provide accounts of such programmes, which are often linked with family centres. Cliffe and Berridge (1991) describe the work of the children's services teams which provide similar services in Warwickshire to supplement the work of area team social workers. Sometimes it is the family aide or home help who offers a caring relationship to a parent. The role of the teacher and the youth worker in providing support for youngsters should not be overlooked either. Regular contact between a young child's teacher and the social worker is important both for assessment purposes, and to help the teacher to carry the strain of offering daily care to a child who may show signs of distress at times of family crisis.

On occasions, usually for short periods but sometimes for extended ones, the social worker in field, day care or residential settings is the only person able to offer a caring and supportive relationship to a youngster or a parent. Sometimes the availability of a supportive relationship, whether with a social worker, a volunteer or a family aide, may enable a parent to give a youngster the loving care which he or she needs. This is particularly so in the case of depressed parents. The work of Brown and Harris (1978) has emphasised the crucial importance of emotional support in the lives of depressed mothers.

Consumer studies make clear that carers, whether they be natural or substitute parents, value a caring, reliable, accessible and efficient service. Jones (1985), reporting on a range of specialist services to families aimed at keeping children out of care or returning them to their families, stresses the importance of services being available when needed, as well as the key role of the social workers in 'keeping the parents, especially the fathers, on the job' (p. 151) and thus available to the family. The intensive family preservation services in America have had some success in keeping very vulnerable families together, including cases where parents abuse drugs or alcohol, by providing a social worker who is available to offer support over a crisis period on a seven-day-a-week, twenty-four-hour-a-day basis if needed (Whittaker *et al.* 1990). On a less intensive basis, family centre workers (Smith 1992) or members of the children's service teams set up by some British authorities (Cliffe and Berridge 1991) can provide emotional support.

Another important element in the relationship between social workers and parents, or other carers, is that of colleague. Consumer studies show that those struggling with the day-to-day task of helping a youngster recover from damaging experiences in the past greatly value the social worker as a sounding-board against whom they can bounce their ideas. While advice is usually valued, they need to know to what extent they are free to reject the advice if it seems inappropriate. Social workers need to remember that there are many different styles of parenting. New families as well as natural families often complain that the workers have not taken enough trouble to understand *their* particular way of doing things, so that they can tailor their advice accordingly, or – better still – so that they and the families can together work out ways of dealing with particular situations or problems. Black families, in particular, complain that white social workers frequently misunderstand their ways of raising their children and underestimate the positive aspects of their cultures, parenting styles and beliefs (see especially Small 1986).

Deeds and services

Jones (1985) found that the most effective models of service in keeping children out of care were those that offered casework together with a range of practical services and advocacy. Hardiker and her colleagues (1991), in a study of preventive child care social work in two English counties, found that psychosocial casework combining emotional and practical help was the major approach to family support work. Check-list 2 expands on the services listed in Schedule 2 of the Children Act and lists some of the practical services which should be considered.

The 'other' category, backed up by Section 17 and Schedule 2 of the Children Act 1989, including the provision of cash assistance, offers much scope for creative social work. One of the most useful services I offered to a single parent mother in a rural area was repeated requests to the driving test authorities to give her an early test when her nervousness led her to fail for the third, fourth and fifth times. Ensuring that a single parent, fearful of violence from a former partner, has a phone in the home (if necessary by using Section 17 money to pay the rental) can offer peace of mind; it may even pay for itself by cutting down on unnecessary social work visits just to deal with a minor query when a phone call would suffice.

Although some authorities had relief care schemes for children with physical or learning disabilities prior to the Children Act 1989, voluntary care used to be the recognised route for other families needing respite care, but, as we have seen, tended to be offered reluctantly or not at all. Non-stigmatised respite care (or as the White Paper leading to the Act called it, 'shared care') should now be a resource available to all families under stress, whatever the reason. Such schemes should involve the child returning to the same carers whenever the service is necessary, rather than, as has so frequently happened, the child going to a different carer on each occasion. Millham *et al.* (1986) found that 22 per cent of their sample who left care had a second admission, and 6 per cent had a third within two years. The findings of Rowe *et al.* (1989) are similar. Respite carers may well be involved with (and should be adequately rewarded for) offering support to a family when the youngsters are living at home. This sort of service is particularly appropriate for parents, especially those living alone, who suffer from recurrent mental disorder, alcohol or drug problems, or need to spend periods away from home, perhaps because of a physical health problem. A team of Lothian social workers, and Barnardo's 'positive options planning scheme' (see Batty 1993) have developed such services for parents who are HIV positive or who have AIDS. Aldgate and her colleagues are presently studying respite care schemes and their guidance on good practice for managers and workers is shortly to be published (Aldgate *et al.* in preparation).

Check-list 2. Deeds or services

Deeds or services	For whom?
Day care/child minder/day foster care	(step) mother
Playgroup/mother and toddler group	(step) father
Help to get into appropriate school	non-resident parent
After school care	each child
Help with further education/literacy/	carer(s)
job/training for parents or adoles-	carers' children
cents	other helpers
Leisure facilities for parents and chil-	
dren	
Practical help	
— household tasks	
— child care/handling	
— baby-sitting	
— help with transport/fares	
— repairs, decoration, gardening	
Respite care	
Holiday for parents, children (together	
or separate)	
Financial aid (regular or one-off grant)	
Material help	
Welfare rights advice and/or advocacy	
Help with a health problem	
Help with a housing problem	
Help with a legal problem	
Debt counselling	
Conciliation/mediation/advocacy –	
with own department	
with DSS	
Housing Department	
School	
Health Service	
Courts	
Creditors	
Members of family	
Supervision	
Other (every case is different!)	

Supervision

Supervision is best seen as a service to children and families, although it impinges on the nature of the relationship and on the therapeutic process. Legal provisions and regulations and guidance under the 1989 Act require that all children who are looked after by the authority, or who are in care but living with parents, should be supervised wherever they are placed. It is also necessary for some children, either living with parents or elsewhere but not in care, to be supervised for their own protection. Sometimes parents, especially if they tend towards impulsive or immature behaviour, need to be supervised to remind them of the agreements that govern the youngsters remaining with them, as well as to allow the supervisors to detect a deteriorating situation for the child. Usually the role of supervisor will be combined with that of helper, but sometimes it may be the only role, as in the case of permanent foster placements that are well established and where the foster family is coping very adequately as a unit.

Problems about the necessity of supervision are likely to be minimised if its purpose, and the way it will be carried out, is discussed at the start of every placement. It should then be discussed at regular intervals, and recorded in written agreements. Although none of us particularly likes being checked-up on, or supervised, we usually accept that it is necessary, and this is normally the case with clients we are required to supervise, whether they be children, natural families or substitute parents. From their interviews with parents Packman *et al.* (1986, p. 210) conclude that:

> Frankly and honestly presented in the context of a genuine concern to help, and as an integral part of that concern – the ultimate safety net – the power to control and compel can be both understandable and even helpful to some parents.

A mother interviewed during my 'home on trial' research said: 'I saw her more as a supervisor. I didn't view her as an interfering old so-and-so. I used to see her as a person who was doing her job – checking-up.' (Thoburn 1980: 93)

Being checked-up on or supervised is more difficult for some people to cope with than others, and this does not only apply to natural families. Some substitute carers give as a major reason for wanting to adopt that this step will mean they are free of social workers interfering in their lives and preventing them from getting on with caring for the children in their own particular way.

Within the constraints of the Children Act regulations, agreed conditions attached to supervision orders, or Section 8 orders about 'specific issues' or 'prohibited steps', the style of supervision needs to be negotiated with all concerned. A pattern should then emerge which ensures the necessary protection for the youngster while interfering as little as possible with the family's established way of living.

The question of physical punishment is an important one which needs to be discussed alongside that of supervision. Physical punishment of children looked after by local authorities is no longer permitted. However, the pages of *Foster Care* magazine have included several letters and articles about children moved from foster homes because of what the authority considered to be an unreasonable punishment. This is an especially important issue when considering placements with families from cultural backgrounds which have a different view about physical punishment, or when considering allegations of abuse when there is a disagreement between parents and social workers about methods of punishment.

Words or therapy

There is now a wide range of therapeutic techniques for helping families, individuals and groups and most of these may have something to offer depending on the circumstances of each case. (See Howe (1987) for a discussion of social work theories for practice and the papers edited by Stevenson (1989) on aspects of practice when there is an issue of child protection.)

A 'task-centred' approach, as described by Doel and Marsh (1992) and Aldgate (1989) emphasises the importance of negotiating agreements about problems to be tackled and methods to be used with the different family members. Within this agreement-based approach a wide range of methods may be helpful.

Because it deals with the 'here and now' – while acknowledging the influence of past events and past relationships on present behaviour and sense of identity – I have found work based on transactional analysis has much to commend it (see Pitman 1984). Among the many models of family therapy, Minuchin's 'ecological' model, which pays particular attention to the impact of the environment on a family's ability to cope, and focuses on work with disorganised families and those in poverty, is particularly relevant to families of children in care (Minuchin 1974). The complexity of most cases involving children at risk of long-term care tends to mean that behavioural social work on its own will rarely be adequate, but behavioural techniques can have a substantial impact if introduced at the appropriate stage. Humanistic or person-centred methods, especially as described by writers such as Jordan (1979) who bring the insights of 'practice wisdom' learned from years of statutory social work practice, must, in my view, form the basis of helping to which other more specialised methods and techniques will be added.

Although individual workers will have their preferred methods there are general principles based on the values to which I have already referred which will guide the choice of method. The 'partnership' model of practice necessitates the availability of a range of social work methods, the one chosen depending on joint discussion of the problems, needs and preferences of the client. It is therefore necessary for social workers to develop skills in describing to their clients the respective merits of different models of helping, and discussing the likelihood of success and the impact and demands made on them, so that families may have some choice about the service. This is in line with the concept of empowerment, and – especially if a longer-term service is involved – is likely to cut down on the risks of unnecessary dependence and passivity.

> Balancing the client's needs for more care with the desire to decrease dependency and minimise the financial burden for the agency may complicate the worker's decision-making on behalf of the client. Empowering parents by means of carefully constructed agreements, in which they fully participate, and by involving them in case conferences so that they may have the information which helps to combat a sense of powerlessness, is a major part of the strategy to prevent unnecessary dependence or a sense of victimisation.
>
> Parents need to be asked if they are satisfied with the way things are progressing. Are there services they would like changed? Is there a different kind of help they would like? (Maluccio *et al.* 1986: 146)

A tendency which should be avoided is for a worker, or a team of workers, deciding on their preferred style of work and the client being expected to fit in with this. Moore (1986, p. 66), talking of child abuse work, warns of the dangers of 'falling into the false position of being so hooked on one method that clients have to respond to that method, instead of selecting a method to fit the client'.

Check-list 3. Words or therapy

With whom and in what combinations?	Offered by whom?
(step) mother	one worker or two?
(step) father	own agency or another?
	social worker or other professional?
non-resident parent	
non-resident parent's children and partner	*Styles of work* (not exhaustive)
	crisis intervention
	counselling — individual
each child	— marital
carer(s)	— bereavement
carers' children	supportive social work
members of extended family	behavioural social work
other members of helping network	social skills work
	life-story work
	task-centred work
	marital/sex therapy
	psychotherapy
	play therapy
	family therapy (which model?)
	transactional analysis
	cognitive therapy
	consciousness-raising
	conciliation
	groupwork
	alone or in combination

It is especially important that statutory powers are not used to avoid consultation with the client about the method of help to be offered, a tendency noted by Dyde (1987) in her discussion of place of safety orders. Voluntary agencies may have more freedom to decide about their model of work if the client is free to either take or leave their services. Statutory agencies, however, should offer a range of services, from family therapy to consciousness-raising groups, and include practical help as well as help with emotional and relationship difficulties.

The specific aspects of providing a service for women, for children and for men, should be considered.

Feminist writers have shown that while women are the most frequent target for social work attention, they are often given an inappropriate service which decreases rather than increases their self-esteem. A model of practice which enhances the sense of identity and self-worth of women, often involving the use of mutual aid groups, is being developed by such writers (see especially McLeod and Dominelli 1982, and Donnelly 1986).

It is even more difficult to find in the social work literature guidance about working effectively with male clients. This is a significant omission, given that it is usually fathers or stepfathers who inflict violence on women and children, and a significant minority of children coming into care do so from single father households. In my study of children who returned home from care (Thoburn 1980), I found that the most distressing 'tug-of-love' cases were those where social workers did not consider the father's potential for caring for his children and consequently placed them in permanent substitute homes when return home to the father should have been considered at a much earlier stage. Millham and his colleagues (1986) have shown that many children in care became separated from their fathers because social workers did not place enough emphasis on keeping them in touch.

Welcome exceptions to this generally poor service offered to male clients is the work being undertaken by conciliation services (Parkinson 1986) and the advocacy-style work undertaken from a family centre by Liffman (1978). Marsh (1991) also gives some thought to working in partnership with fathers, and the *Access* magazine of the organisation Families need Fathers is another important source of information.

There are two other areas of special concern to child care social workers, and to which social work theorists have been slow to turn their attention. The first is work aimed at alleviating the special problems of stepfamilies (see Brown 1982, and Robinson 1991). The National Stepfamily Association is beginning to fill some of the gaps. The second is the more systematic development of social work theories and methods which are appropriate to the needs of members of minority ethnic groups (see Ahmed *et al.* 1986, and Dominelli 1988).

Working directly with children and young people

Despite excellent pioneering work with children which is now widely reported in journal articles, books and on video, children, especially those below adolescence, are rarely given a service in their own right. Children too are fellow citizens and a child of whatever age has a right to social work service, the principles of which are the same as for adults. Insofar as they are able, children should be partners in the decisions about how they are to be helped and where they should be placed. There should be an agreed protection plan for all children at risk; and for those whose long-term needs are not being adequately met, there must be a clear plan for their future.

Research has shown that the wellbeing of such children depends not only on meeting the basic physical and psychological needs which they share with all children, but on the provision of a 'sense of permanence' and also a sense of their own 'identity' (see Figure 1). These two must be kept in balance if the youngster is to develop the sense of self-worth which is essential for satisfying relationships in the future. The work of Rutter and her colleagues (1983) in looking at the parenting abilities of youngsters brought up in residential care shows that there is a greater risk of disturbed relationships with future partners, but especially with children, when these needs are not met. It is important to note that it is a *sense* of permanence which is crucial, rather than a particular legal permanence option such as adoption, a point made strongly by Lahti and her colleagues

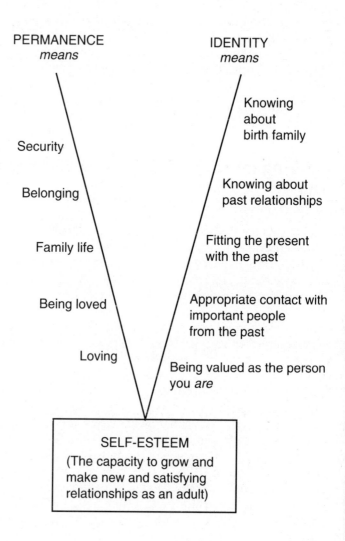

Figure 1.   The special needs of children who are looked after by the local authority

(1982) monitoring the search for permanent placements for 259 children in Oregon.

A sense of identity can best be achieved by continued contact with parents and other members of the natural family and with other people who have cared for – or about – a youngster in the past. (I return to this important point in the next chapter.) If continued contact is ruled out, skilled social work, including work on a child's life history, can be a help, but is no substitute for actual contact when it comes to dealing with the fantasies with which some children, and indeed some adoptive or foster families, become preoccupied.

Black children should be encouraged to have pride in their colour, race and culture, and need help in coping with racism. If contact with natural families is not possible for them, they at least need contact with their own community and culture, which can obviously be best achieved by placement with carers coming from the same background.

Care is also needed to ensure that young people's sexual orientation is respected, and that they feel safe to discuss their developing sexuality – whether heterosexual or homosexual – with carers and social workers.

There are no better guides to the essential principles for working with children than Winnicott's 1964 lecture 'Face to face with children' (recently reprinted by BAAF, 1986), and Donley's 'Ten commandments for working with children' (Donley 1975: 20–22). Two points which I will emphasise here are that anyone working with children must find ways of coping with the pain which allowing them to express their hurt will cause; and you won't have to mind sometimes feeling rather silly or stupid. I remember sitting on a lawn with many eyes looking on from the surrounding houses, addressing a youngster who I thought was still hiding behind the hedge, only to discover eventually that he was no longer there. And on many occasions risking a guess as to what a silent child might be feeling only to receive a look of scorn at my stupidity – which might have meant that I was wide of the mark, or else too close for comfort and had to be sent packing before I made a dent in the invisible wall around her.

There are many techniques from the various branches of social work, youth work and play therapy which offer useful tools – from social skills work and role-playing, which may help youngsters to practise a 'cover story' to explain why they are changing schools, to the use of consciousness-raising groups along the lines of the 'Who Cares?' groups. The technique of life-story work, described by Ryan and Walker (1985) and illustrated in the videos 'Taking the lid off' and 'In touch with children', can be used with children living with their birth families as well as those moving to substitute families. Wilson and her colleagues (1992) have recently produced a practical text on non-directive play therapy, and Aldgate and her colleagues (1989) give guidance on working with adolescents in foster care.

A word of warning, though. Although you will occasionally totally fail to break through the protective wall which some youngsters erect, more often you will become a very important person to the youngster, who will very much want to please you. Since your job is to help prepare a plan which you believe has most chance of meeting the child's needs, there is some risk that your enthusiasm for the plan will communicate itself in such a way that he or she will be reluctant to express any doubts. The point was brought home forcibly during our recent research when several youngsters whose workers were convinced that they wished to be adopted, conveyed to the research psychologist that they had severe doubts. Most of them managed to sabotage their proposed placements before they actually moved in! If there is a possibility that a child is not totally convinced of a particular plan, or if the advantages of several options are evenly balanced, it may be appropriate to bring in an independent psychologist to help to assess what he or she is really saying. Morris (1984) offers some useful advice on how to recognise what children are trying to tell us, and warns of the dangers of not listening carefully enough.

The introduction of guardians *ad litem* has brought a measure of protection, but they often become involved after a placement has been made and other options have been closed. It is also regrettable that the child is not normally a party in adoption and matrimonial proceedings. In such circumstances, if, as the accountable social worker, you are aware of any doubts in anyone's mind about the appropriateness of adoption, it is important to alert the court so that a guardian *ad litem* can be appointed at an early stage in the proceedings instead of a reporting officer. The group reviewing adoption law has recommended that guardians *ad litem* should normally be appointed in adoption proceedings, and there is a continuing discussion following the implementation of the Children Act 1989 about how best to ensure that children's views are available to the courts in matrimonial cases. The new 'family assistance order' brings the possibility of a short period of focused social work to help divorcing parents who are in serious conflict to minimise the harm done to the children.

The management of child placement

Three related and important themes running through recent studies of social work practice in general, and child care work in particular, are: the effective management of services; quality assurance and control; and the desirability of planning for permanence in order to avoid children drifting through a succession of unplanned placements.

A consistent response to the findings of recent child abuse inquires has been to set up systems to ensure that social workers follow departmental policies and detailed instructions. Many departments have also responded managerially to research findings about poor planning for children in care and have set up panels of managers and senior workers to make decisions about children. Although such devices might ensure a more even service, and protect some clients from poor social work practice, they have the major disadvantage of taking decisions further away from the family members themselves, thus making it more difficult to achieve the partnership model of social work practice.

Vernon and Fruin (1986), Howe (1986) and Packman *et al.* (1986) comment on the paradox of social workers having considerable autonomy to make decisions about children either directly or indirectly through their control of information to the organisation and to the consumers, and yet feeling themselves to be powerless. All the studies show that the complexity of the situations confronted makes it very difficult to draw up detailed regulations. England (1986, p. 68) sees this as a fundamental problem for social work agencies and one of the reasons for low morale which characterises many departments. 'It is the doublebind; the agency must protect its interests by structuring the work, but in doing so it disables the competent worker and inhibits the development of truly articulate and accomplished practice.'

Elsewhere (Thoburn 1986) I have argued that quality control in child care *must* rely largely on professional mechanisms such as training and consultation within the context of general policy guidelines and a system for inspection, consumer involvement and complaint. Lack of clarity as to whether the social worker is empowered to take professional decisions, or is simply the collector of information and implementer of decisions taken at a more senior level, leads to confusion about the nature of supervision and consultation needed. If decisions are to be taken jointly with parents and children, in the light of the individual circumstances in each case, the major responsibility for those decisions must fall on the case-accountable social worker or workers in consultation with the team leader and others who have relevant information. Thus planning panels, reviews and case conferences are important either as 'fail-safe' mechanisms checking that plans *are* being made and good work carried out; or for pooling information and stimulating lateral thinking about ways of helping. They must not, however, hold up the day-to-day planning of the workers, parents, young people, carers and first line supervisors or team leaders.

The key role of the team leader of child care workers has been emphasised by many of the researchers and also by the authors of the Beckford Report (London Borough of Brent 1985). Rowe, in her summary of the research findings, comments that 'supervision as seen in these studies did not seem to offer either real support or appropriate control', and deplores the current moves 'to turn supervisors into team managers [which] may help to achieve control, but offer little hope of the more effective support which is vital to improving practice' (DHSS 1985: 19).

The stressful nature of the decisions to be made means that adequate support and consultation, as well as supervision, is essential to an effective child placement service. The appointment of child abuse consultants is a welcome step forward in meeting the need for consultation on specific cases at specific times. It is, however, no substitute for the availability on a regular basis of a trusted and knowledgeable colleague or consultant (who may be, but need not necessarily be, the team leader) who is familiar with the cases, acts as a sounding-board against whom ideas can be bounced, and above all helps the worker to face up to the pain of caring about people in distress while retaining the objectivity necessary to work and plan appropriately. Family therapists recognise this and organise their work in support teams, which is perhaps not unconnected with the growing popularity of this model of practice. Those using other models of social work practice could learn from their experience and insist on similar support and consultation facilities, which are now rarely available outside specialist units, usually in the voluntary sector.

Emergency services

Another important aspect of agency policy concerns the provision of an out-of-hours service, and cover when the worker known to the children and those caring for them is unavailable. Effective child care work involves the taking of risks and, at times, the acceptance of acute pressure on non-professionals, whether they be foster carers, adopters, family aides, volunteer befrienders, relatives or the parents and the children themselves. Moments of stress cannot be expected to confine themselves to office hours. Mattinson and Sinclair (1979), in describing their attempts to provide marital therapy to high risk families, who were clients of a social services department, graphically illustrate the obstacles to providing consistent service within a bureaucratic framework. Packman *et al.* (1986) and Millham *et al.* (1986) have shown that a high proportion of children come into care on place of safety orders, often taken out of office hours and often by the police, thus frustrating the attempts of the social worker to maintain children within their families.

Reliable, purposeful and caring social work during office hours greatly diminishes the need for clients, even those under considerable stress, to call for an emergency service. However, most specialist unit workers do provide a home phone number, or a duty system based on a worker known to the client or carer being available out of office hours. The families taking special needs children whom we interviewed (Thoburn *et al.* 1986) told us that such a service greatly reduced their anxiety, even though they rarely used it. Paradoxically such a service is more likely to be available to those such as foster parents and adopters who have more than average coping resources, than to natural or stepfamilies experiencing severe difficulties with their children.

Local authority workers are frequently discouraged from giving their home phone number to clients and few authorities are willing to pay the phone rental, even for workers undertaking high risk social work. Where an adequate duty system is not available (and it is a minority of authorities who provide an out-of-hours *social work* service as opposed to a rather grudging emergency service), the worker knowing that a client is under stress is left with the very difficult decision of how to provide out-of-hours support.

Although workers who are inadequately supported and often placed under considerable stress during their working time should not be expected to be available as a matter of routine outside office hours, I consider that it is the duty of managers and workers involved in child care work (or, for that matter, work with other vulnerable people), to take all possible steps to ensure an adequate emergency duty system. Such a system should, at a minimum, be accessible to clients and adopt a welcoming as opposed to a deterrent approach. There should be the possibility of access to records, at least on those clients or carers identified as being under severe stress, and the accountable social worker should be able to leave messages about any imminent difficulties and suggested ways of handling them. There should be encouragement for emergency duty workers to try to get hold of the social worker who knows the case for advice about handling any crisis which may occur.

To summarise, the social work service to children and those who care for or about them should be efficient but also intimate and accessible, with as much authority as possible being delegated to the professional workers and to the parents, carers and children themselves. The authors of *Direct Work with Families* (Miller and Cook 1981) describe the philosophy of Family Service Units in attempting to offer the client a relationship with the whole agency, rather than simply with the accountable worker, a philosophy which also underlies the approach of most 'permanent placement' units (Thoburn *et al.* 1986, Thoburn 1990). Such an approach goes some way towards meeting the worker's need for consultation and support and the client's need for a consistent approach to problems even when the accountable worker is not available.

4 Choosing the placement

Having considered what we know about the sort of children who may need placements in care, and the general principles guiding the work to be undertaken, the chapters which follow offer practical guidance on how to make decisions about the placement and about the social work and other services to be offered.

The major decisions are:

- Should the child leave home and be looked after by the local authority?
- If not, what services are necessary to ensure that he or she receives good enough care and is protected from harm?
- Will the provision of appropriate services require court intervention or the use of child protection procedures?
- If the child needs to leave home, are there more suitable alternatives to being looked after by the local authority, such as placement with relatives, possibly supported by Section 17 money, and possibly formalised by the use of a Section 8 residence order?
- If being looked after by the local authority is necessary, what legal route is appropriate?
- Which placement will best meet the needs of the child, and if long-term provision may be needed, is a 'bridge' or 'assessment' placement necessary in the first instance?
- What legal status for any new placement will be appropriate?
- What should be the nature of contact between the youngster,

the birth parents, relatives or previous carers and how is the placement and social work service to facilitate such contact?

- What is the nature of the social work and other services to be offered to the child, the birth parents or relatives, the previous carers and the new carers?
- What practical and financial support will be needed to maximise the chance that the placement will meet the needs of the child?

I consider now the social work service at the assessment stage. This may be assessment before children come into care, or assessment at times in their care careers when a change of plan is necessary.

Assessment and prevention

The research described in Chapters 1 and 2 confirms my view that the aim of 'prevention' should not be just the narrow one of preventing children coming into care, but the prevention of the total breakdown of family relationships alongside the prevention of physical harm, and the minimising of emotional harm to the youngster. (Since I am not covering the important issues of primary prevention here, that is, the provision of universal services to meet the needs of all children for decent housing, adequate food, clothing, educational and recreational opportunities, but rather considering those children who are seriously at risk of long-term separation from their parents, some degree of emotional damage is almost inevitable and the task is to minimise and as far as possible repair such damage.) The BASW code of practice on prevention and rehabilitation offers a framework for the provision of appropriate services (BASW 1987), and more practical advice is offered in the chapters edited by Gibbons (1992) and by Marsh and Triseliotis (1993).

Assessment is a central part of prevention, and a high quality preventive service paves the way for good decisions and effective practice if leaving home becomes necessary. The Department of Health guidance on undertaking a comprehensive assessment (DH 1988) gives an agenda for such an assessment, though it needs to be set in a framework of theory and values and not used mechanically in a series of question and answer sessions. A set of papers edited by Adcock and White (1991) gives guidance on the meaning of 'significant harm' as used in the 1989 Act.

Switching gear: preparation for care

Experienced workers will be familiar with the stage in family social work where it becomes a distinct possibility that children's needs may best be met by being cared for away from home for more than short respite periods. It is essential to acknowledge this stage with the family members and discuss the advantages and disadvantages of a stay away from home for each child. This may be after many months of social work with the family, or it may be at the first interview. Even after implementation of the Children Act 1989, students and social workers tell me that they hesitate to discuss care or accommodation with families because departmental policy is often opposed to this course of action. This obviously leads to the counter-productive interviews described by Fisher and his colleagues (1986) as workers strove not to 'hear' that the parents were asking for their children to be looked after, and parents blocked their ears to the workers' attempts to persuade them of the disadvantages of separation.

I have found that, after a long account by parents of how bad everything is, the question 'Are you asking me to find somewhere else for Jenny to live for a while?' allows us to get down to the real work of discussing ways of helping. In cases where a child may be at risk of harm, it is equally important to say at an early stage 'Do you think that I have come here to take Billy away from you?', followed by a discussion about whether this is a likely possibility. Without such statements, productive discussion is frustrated by the hidden agenda of a youngster's leaving home, or being compulsorily removed.

After working for some time with a family, the question mark may be in your mind – but as far as you know not in the mind of the family. It seems more honest, and will be more productive, to say something like, 'We've been working at this problem for a long time, and I'm beginning to feel that we should seriously discuss whether it wouldn't be better if Jack were looked after away from home.'

Fisher and his colleagues (1986) have indicated that families who perceive that their wishes are not going to be acknowledged and given due weight, have to escalate or exaggerate their problems in order to get over to the worker that they are serious about their request for care away from home. If not yet convinced of the need, I find it helpful to say to such families something like: 'I know you don't find it easy to ask for this, and that you have tried very hard to avoid it, so you must feel it is the only way out of your difficulties. However, I have only just met you, and I need time to talk over with you whether it really will help, and if so how we should best go about it. If you will work with me on this, and you still end up feeling that a placement away from home is the best way to deal with things, then I promise, you that that is what will happen.' Such a statement, of course, requires the worker to have the power to make such a promise, and if such authority is not delegated she should discuss it with her team leader and say that she wants support for this course of action. If, as in some authorities, the actual decision lies with a panel, or senior manager, the worker must explain this to the family and say that she will go with them to help them make their case if that is what they still think is appropriate after fully exploring the situation.

In such circumstances it is important to have an agreement about how long this assessment process will take, and what it will involve. Sometimes it will need intensive work for several hours in the course of a single day, perhaps using the facilities of a family centre. More often it will extend over a period of days or weeks. Sometimes residential care for the whole family is appropriate, especially if a child might not otherwise be safe. The Family Rights Group keeps an up-to-date list of residential units for the whole family.

All too often research tells us that social workers refuse to consider looking after a child at this stage and thus miss an important opportunity for planning. Such a stance frequently provokes families – who see no other alternative – into forcing the worker's hand by creating a crisis. Crisis admissions, as we have already seen, are rarely in the interests of children or parents.

Leaving home
Check-list 4 shows how much ground has to be covered before

or shortly after a youngster comes into care or is accommodated. It makes a great deal of sense to start on these processes as soon as leaving home becomes a real possibility, even if in the event it does not become necessary. Talking about the realities – where the youngster will live, what sort of regime will be involved, what the contact arrangements will be, how the parents will feel about seeing someone else caring for their child – preferably with the potential care-givers, as well as the social worker, gives parents and children the information they need if they are to be fully committed to the eventual decision about placement. It is regrettable that many agencies organise their child care, especially placements in residential care, in such a way that it is extremely difficult to give parents, children and, indeed, individual social workers a real choice about placement. Clearly the earlier discussions start about the nature of the placement, the more possible will it be to have some choice.

It is also important at this stage to discuss the legal routes into care or accommodation, and again, insofar as it is in the interests of the child, to give all concerned as much choice as possible about the appropriate route. If long-term care is a real possibility, the various alternatives must be considered, from adoption on the one hand to a defined length of stay in a therapeutic unit or professional foster home on the other; from voluntary accommodation to use of 'freeing' for adoption procedures. DH regulations and guidance make it clear that adoption should now be considered as a possibility for any child coming into long-term care, and equally the Adoption Agencies' Regulations (1983) make clear that parents should be informed of the range of placements available, and the legal routes towards meeting the child's needs. A placement, perhaps with relatives or others known to the family, and perhaps with a view to an application for a residence order, is yet another possibility to be discussed.

Normally, however, the discussions will centre on the advantages and disadvantages of accommodation or a court order. The practice reported by research writers of refusing parents' requests for voluntary care, and then waiting until the situation deteriorates enough for a place of safety (emergency protection) order to be obtainable, can surely not be in the interests of children. Whilst clearly very young children at risk of abuse should not be left with parents whilst waiting for a court hearing, it

Check-list 4. Moving into accommodation or care

NB. This is a *process* which will take time – the order of proceeding will vary.

Give information (verbal and recorded) about:

- process, and likely emotional and practical impact on all concerned
- legal situation (advise to consult a solicitor if appropriate)
- alternative legal routes to care/consequences of prolonged stay
- placement – preferably a choice made by visiting more than one placement if appropriate
- financial consequences

Use easily readable material and leave all relevant forms for them to look over. You will need to repeat things. The Department of Health leaflets are extremely clear and helpful, as is Harlow Parents' Aid booklet, and the FRG/NSPCC booklet. The material should be in the languages of the local community, and should be recorded in such a way as to be accessible to those with a literacy problem, or with a sensory impairment.

Gather information about facts and feelings on:

- all concerned, especially child, siblings, both parents, step-parents, significant relatives
- child's history and any health and genetic factors
- detailed information on child to help care-givers (e.g. food, skin care, and fears – e.g. of dark, for young child words used for lavatory, etc.)

Ask for photos – to help child during separation, and possibly life-story work.

Complete any necessary forms, and do preliminary work on contents of placement agreement (see Guidance and Regulations, Volume 3).

- Collect medical history and note/chart any illnesses, accidents or injuries.
- Explain significance of any signature, e.g. re medical treatment.
- Complete financial assessment forms. Advise on what to do about child benefit, disability allowance, income support, child support payment, etc.
- Explain legal requirements to keep in touch.
- If child will be looked after for some time explain your obligation to safeguard the welfare of the child.
- Explain your obligation to offer a counselling service to *both* parents if there is any question of adoption. Need to discuss all alternatives. Need for information about other parent if living elsewhere, and anyone else who has parental responsibility.
- Carefully record all the detailed information collected on the child's and family's history. Complete a family tree, and chart the child's relationships and movements.

Introductory visits for child and parents/significant others. Note value of care-giver visiting family home. Discussion of visiting plan. Do parents need transport/fares/emotional support? (Discuss names to be used, make sure that the parents know what you have told care-giver.)

- Discuss and formulate agreed plan for future social work support to parents, child, care-givers. How is the plan and social work service going to be recorded? What are expectations of all concerned? How can the plan be changed? What contingencies do you and others have in mind if the plan does not work? What notice should the parent or older child give if they wish to end the placement? Under what circumstances will the social worker remove the child against the wishes of others? What is the departmental complaints procedure?

Draw up written agreements with all involved in making the placement work. (See Guidance and Regulations, Volume 3. The forms provided by FRG and NFCA are consistent with the guidance.)

- Discuss what clothing, toys, medicines, children are to take with them.

- Explain need for pre-placement medical and make arrangements for this.
- Discuss process of admission. Who should take child? Pros and cons of parents going with social worker.
- Discuss a 'cover story' with parents and older children.

Inform school/EWO/Health Visitor of change

- Arrange new school. Discuss child with new teacher, preferably jointly with carers and parents. Discuss registration with new GP if necessary.
- Check whether carers need money urgently, e.g. to buy clothes. Get emergency payment, if necessary.
- Arrange next visits to parents, child, carers, and how parent is to know how child has settled.
- Arrange first review.
- Put parents in touch with a 'Families of children in care' group if there is one and they would like extra support.

All this applies also when a care order or emergency protection order is in force:

- Convene child protection conference if appropriate and prepare family members for attendance.
- Discuss case with local authority solicitor; prepare statement of evidence.
- Advise and if necessary help parents to see a solicitor.
- Be available to discuss case with guardian *ad litem.*
- Prepare parents, children and care-givers for court. Tell them what you are likely to say in court and go over the contents of any reports with them.
- In consultation with supervisor make clear plan to present to court for safeguarding the child's welfare. Rehearse your evidence with a colleague acting as 'devil's advocate'.

---

ought to be possible for children to remain at home until care proceedings can be initiated more often than is currently the case. Early statistics following implementation of the Children

Act show that far fewer emergency orders are being applied for. This period before a hearing, as well as allowing the guardian *ad litem* to take a fresh look at the situation, will allow for discussions about what will happen if the court finds that placement away from home is necessary. Preliminary work towards an appropriate placement can then be undertaken.

Whether accommodation or a care order is being considered, it is important at this stage to give parents as much information as possible in a form in which they can most easily absorb it, and to be available to explain, or to refer the family to someone else who may be able to explain, the position, such as a solicitor, a parents' aid group or law centre. The Family Rights Group and NSPCC (1992) have jointly produced a guide for parents, and Harlow Parents' Aid produces a similar booklet. One of these should be given to all parents, complemented by information about the agency in question and the Department of Health short leaflets on the Children Act produced for parents and children. Any forms and explanatory leaflets should be left with the family to read without the social worker breathing down their necks, before they are asked to sign them. The FRG/NSPCC booklet is produced in several languages, and the help of a disability worker should be sought in communicating with parents or children who have a sight or hearing impairment. Sensitivity to the needs of parents who are illiterate is essential.

It may well be that if proceedings are being initiated against the parents' wishes, and especially if an emergency protection order or child assessment order has been necessary, they will be angry with the worker. It is nonetheless important, if at all possible, for the same worker to continue to offer them help. There are occasions, however, when the strength of feeling is such that a second worker may need to be involved, or where it may be appropriate to ensure that the parents have other support from someone they trust, such as from a parents' aid group or from a volunteer.

General principles covering choice of placement

Check-list 5 has been devised to help social workers and guardians *ad litem* to make sense of the volume of information, often conflicting, which needs to guide the choice of placement. Even when a family is known to the worker and the arguments for and against the child leaving home have been well rehearsed, it is still rarely possible to know how parents and child will react to separation and therefore to make a long-term or permanent placement straight from home. Vernon and Fruin (1986) and, more recently, Cliffe and Berridge (1991) show how the initial placement was rarely one of choice and that the people involved in caring for the youngster initially had a very significant impact on future plans for the child. In particular, if he or she seemed to have settled well, plans for rehabilitation were dropped. Whilst Rowe and her colleagues (1984) have shown that placements originally intended to be short-term which eventually become long-term can be surprisingly satisfactory, Millham *et al.* (1986) indicate that many such placements subsequently break down.

The finding of Berridge and Cleaver (1987) that there was a lower breakdown rate amongst long-term foster children who had been placed after a stay of up to a year in residential care, encourages me in my view that interim or 'bridge' placements with relatives or in residential or foster care are almost always necessary.

Although foster care will normally be appropriate for younger children, and residential care used more often for older teenagers (especially if accommodation away from home is being used as an appropriate route towards independence), it should be possible in the interests of individual children to depart from this formula. The writers of the Beckford Report (London Borough of Brent 1985) suggest that even for young children specialist residential facilities may sometimes be preferable to foster care. Aldgate (1980) has also indicated that residential care may be preferable if return home seems a realistic possibility, since visiting for the natural parents is often more comfortable and therefore easier to sustain if the youngsters are in residential care. The Barnardo's 'Cambridge cottage project' (Fratter *et al.* 1982), the Catholic Children's Society's family makers unit (see Central Television video: 'Taking the lid off') and the Children's Society (Fitzgerald *et al.* 1982) have demonstrated that residential care can provide an excellent base for helping children to move to permanent new families.

Although there will always be a need for emergency reception facilities, both in residential and foster care, elaborate and expensive residential and assessment units are less necessary in view of the increased availability of community assessment facilities such as family centres. Many authorities now have specialist fostering schemes, which go by a variety of names – such as, 'bridge', 'link', 'therapeutic', 'professional'. The earlier schemes tended to be for adolescents (see Cooper 1978, Hazel 1981, and Shaw and Hipgrave 1983) or for children with severe learning disabilities. More recently special schemes for children who have been physically or sexually abused have been set up. Specialist family placement workers have pioneered 'bridge' fostering schemes to provide temporary homes for those whose permanent placements have been disrupted and help the youngsters to move on to another family. Some local authorities have linked foster parents to day care and assessment facilities such as family centres, or to residential units. Cliffe and Berridge (1991) describe the children's services teams set up by Warwickshire to provide placements and family support services after the closure of all the children's homes in the county.

The development of a range of resources is to be welcomed as they allow time for appropriate long-term decisions to be made and carried into effect. However, many are quite unrealistic about time-limits placed on the stay (sometimes as short as three months) and have thus inherited the problems of the former observation and assessment centres – that moves become necessary as time-limits are up. If it proves impossible for a youngster to return home within an agreed time-limit, it can take up to two years to find a permanent new family for a 'harder-to-place' child. Cliffe and Berridge noted the built-in movement because of unrealistically short time restrictions on foster care placements.

Short-term foster care has received too little attention and has either not been included in research studies, or has been included together with long-term fostering. Only recently has awareness of the large numbers of moves of children led to research and practice guidance on short-term care in its own right. The National Foster Care Association with its magazine *Foster Care* and training packs such as 'The challenge of foster care', has stimulated interest in, and greater self-esteem among, foster carers. Research studies such as those of Berridge and Cleaver (1987), Rowe *et al.* (1989) and Cliffe and Berridge (1991) still show that there is too much movement of children during the period when long-term plans are being made or work is being

---

Check-list 5. Placement options

What are the child's needs:

- security?
- continuity?
- special care because of learning or physical disabilities, or emotional problems?
- therapy?
- family life?
- special educational needs?
- to stay in touch with important people from the past
    — parents?
    — siblings?
    — relatives?
    — previous carers?
- to be placed with any/all siblings?
- to remain in touch with friends/go to same school?
- religious upbringing?
- racial/cultural identity?
- any others

What are the child's wishes and views about how these needs should be met?
What are the wishes of each natural parent, anyone else with parental responsibility and any close relatives who are important to the child?
What are the wishes of present care-givers?
What are the legal requirements in respect of child, natural parents, care-givers:

1 Legislation on adoption, residence, and other Section 8 orders, contact?
2 Court rules?
3 Adoption Agencies' Regulations (LAC 84.3, esp. paras. 4 and 37)?
4 Children Act Guidance and Regulations?

What is Departmental policy:
- on child placement alternatives?

- on allowances and maintenance?
- on freeing for adoption, applications to dispense with parental consent to adoption?
- on agreement of a placement panel?

What is your view about how the welfare of the child can best be promoted? Remember to think about the implications of what you do in the next week or so for the child's *long-term* wellbeing.

In many cases the answers to these questions will not all point to the same conclusion.

If your recommendations will result in any of the child's needs not being met; in aspects of the child's or the parent's wishes having to be overruled; or in departmental policy or guidelines or statutory codes not being followed, give in each case the evidence to support that recommendation:

- research findings
- 'practice wisdom'
- knowledge of how the child has reacted in the past
- knowledge of the child's temperament, beliefs and likely reactions to stress resulting from one course of action rather than another
- knowledge of intended substitute parents' temperament, beliefs, likely reactions to stress resulting from one course rather than another
- knowledge of natural parent(s)' temperaments, beliefs, likely reactions to stress resulting from one course rather than another

---

undertaken to return them safely back home. In training events with local authorities, I emphasise the importance of short-term foster carers by saying that 'you can't have a permanence policy without a fostering policy'. A few local authorities have acknowledged the highly skilled and often stressful nature of all short-term fostering tasks by paying fees on top of the maintenance rate, and allowing for paid breaks for all their short-term carers. Sellick (1992) describes the different aspects of support for foster carers, from adequate financial reward and insurance to peer group support. Of particular relevance to child placement workers is his exploration of the roles and tasks of the child's social worker and the carers' link worker.

Assessing individual needs

Given time to make appropriate decisions about long-term placement, it becomes possible to assemble the information necessary. In the course of my research I have looked through many referrals for permanent placement. Workers tend to concentrate on the personal needs and handicaps of the youngster, but in my experience there are two other important dimensions as well. The first is age; we have already noted that over 60 per cent of children being looked after by local authorities are over ten. The second dimension is the nature of the relationships with important others, especially birth parents and siblings. Thus a decision about placement needs to acknowledge at least three dimensions (see Figures 2 and 3 and check-lists 6 and 7).

We may thus be able to get a rough idea about the *sort of placement* which *might* be appropriate. However, further questions need to be asked about the temperament and wishes of the youngsters, of their natural parents or close relatives and of those who are currently caring for them. It will sometimes be the

Check-list 6. Problems/special needs of children

	Age
Physical disability	
Chronic illness	0–2
Severe learning disability	2–4
Down's syndrome	5–10
Learning difficulties	11–14
Behaviour problems	15+
Emotional problems	
Institutionalised	
Lacking in trust due to multiple moves	
Physically abused	
Sexually abused	
Special cultural/racial needs	

N.B. also 'temperament' of child, parents, carers.
Ability to cope with stress or uncertainty

Check-list 7. Relationships with and attitudes of significant others

---

Parent(s) *requesting* adoption residence order/fostering
Parent(s) *consenting/not consenting* to adoption
Parent(s) *consenting/not consenting* to 'permanent' fostering
Parent(s) *consenting/not consenting* to residence order
Parent(s) attached/ambivalently attached/not attached to child
Child attached/ambivalently attached/not attached to parents
Child attached/ambivalently attached/not attached – to siblings or other relatives living elsewhere
Child attached/ambivalently attached/not attached – to siblings with whom he/she is living
Relatives or siblings attached to child
Child attached to present care-givers who do/do not wish him/her to move to a permanent family elsewhere

---

case, especially with older children or sibling groups, that a placement can not be found to meet all a youngster's needs; we then have the difficult task of deciding where compromises can or can not be made. Siblings may wish and need to stay together, but what if one has a physical disability which means that the new parents must have special skills or attributes which are not easily to be found? A black youngster may need to be placed with a family of the same race *and* religion, and may also have a physical or mental disability which requires special care. How long do you wait for the right family? A youngster may need to stay in touch with members of the birth family, but she may already be living with substitute parents to whom she is attached and who say that they can not cope with face-to-face parental contact. Or the natural parents may be temperamentally unable to play the 'aunt and uncle', rather than parent role, and would threaten the stability of the placement if face-to-face contact continued. Research findings seem to point to the fact that the two 'needs' which are least often met are those for placement with a family of the same race, culture, or religion, and for continued contact with members of the birth family. It is this latter important issue to which I now turn.

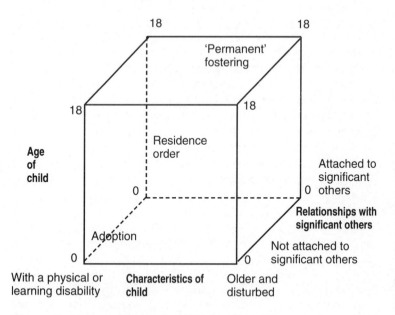

Figure 2. A three-dimensional way of looking at permanent family placement options

Decisions about contact with birth parents, siblings and other previous carers

All these factors will have an impact not only on the decision about the placement, but also about the nature of continued contact and legal status. These issues will be covered in more detail in succeeding chapters, but it is appropriate here to offer some guidance about contact since this will have an effect on the choice of placement. As mentioned earlier all studies of children who are unable to be brought up by their original parents, strongly support the idea that there are two essential elements in enhancing their wellbeing: a sense of being loved and belonging with a family to whom the child feels fully attached (a sense of permanence), and a sense of identity, which is best achieved by continued contact with important people from the past, especially birth parents and other relatives.

All studies which have specifically assessed the wellbeing of

LEGAL CATEGORIES:

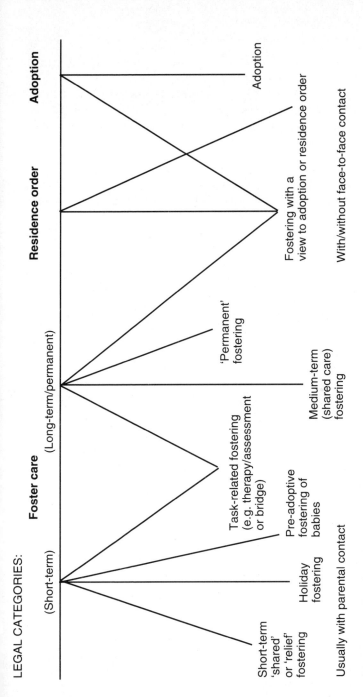

Figure 3. Family placement 'careers'*

*Adapted from British Association of Social Workers (1982), *Guidelines for Practice in Family Placement*

children in long-term foster care have concluded that in the majority of cases wellbeing is enhanced if the children have regular contact with their birth families. From a study of 640 children in long-term care in New York, in which wellbeing, educational performance, behaviour and sense of attachment were examined after children had been away from home for five years, Fanshel and Shinn (1978) concluded:

> In the main we strongly support the notion that continued contact with parents, even when the functioning of the latter is marginal, is good for most foster children. Our data suggest that total abandonment by parents is associated with evidence of emotional turmoil in the children. We can think of no more profound insult to a child's personality than evidence that the parent thinks so little of the relationship with him that there is no motivation to visit and see how he is faring. ... It is our view that the parents continue to have significance for the child even when they are no longer visible to him.

> At the same time we are saying that continued visiting by parents who are long-term wards of the foster care system, while beneficial, is not without stress. It is not easy for children to juggle with two sets of relationships, and the case workers reported that some children showed signs of strain in the process. We maintain, however, that this is a healthier state of affairs than that faced by the child who must reconcile questions about his own worth as a human being with the fact of parental abandonment. In the main, children are more able to accept additional, concerned and loving parental figures in their lives, with all the confusions inherent in such a situation, than to accept the loss of meaningful figures. (Fanshel and Shinn 1978: 487–88)

More recently, Maluccio and his colleagues (1986, pp. 79–80) highlight

> the crucial importance of the biological family in the growth and functioning of children in placement. ... Workers should therefore view the goal of preserving family ties as a major imperative in child care. ... A key means of accomplishing the goal of maintaining family ties is through consistent parental visiting of children in care.

Official guidance in Britain has consistently given a similar message. The 1976 *Foster Care: A Guide to Practice* and the 1983 *Code of Practice on Access to Children in Care* were precursors of the guidance on the Children Act 1989 which states:

Section 8 of the Children Act 1989 makes provision for Contact Orders for children who are *not* in care (including children who are accommodated or adopted), and Section 34 and the Regulations in Volume 3 make provision for contact with children who are in care.

The DH publication (1989b) *Principles and Practice in Regulations and Guidance* states:

> Family links should be actively maintained through visits and other forms of contact. Both parents are important even if one of them is no longer in the family home and fathers should not be overlooked or marginalised ...
>
> Continuity of relationships is important, and attachments should be respected, sustained and developed (p. 9).

This guidance also talks of the importance of contact with relatives, and the value of telephone calls and letters even when actual contact is not possible.

The conclusion to be drawn therefore is that regular contact should continue unless there are reasons to curtail it; it is the best predictor of children returning home. Even when it is decided that children will grow up with permanent substitute parents, though, it is likely that regular contact will enhance their wellbeing – except, that is, in cases where children are totally rejected by their parents, or where older children consistently reject the parents, perhaps as a result of deliberate or emotional ill-treatment.

If parents of young children are unable or unwilling to offer them a permanent home, yet are also unable to accept their need to settle and grow to love substitute parents and therefore consistently attempt to undermine any such placement, it may regrettably be necessary to terminate face-to-face contact, although doors should usually be kept open by indirect two-way contact. Such decisions should be taken on the basis of actions rather than words, since many birth parents – in their anger and despair – will say they are unable to accept something whilst nevertheless not actually behaving in a destructive way. There is no evidence to support the view which is sometimes expressed that continued contact with natural parents prevents children from becoming attached to new parents, other than in the minority of cases where original parents deliberately set out to wreck a placement.

The factor which *is* likely to prevent attachment is when a child has been severely damaged by earlier experiences. Millham and his colleagues (1986) and Berridge and Cleaver (1987), in considering placement breakdowns, found that in only a small minority of cases did parental contact contribute towards the breakdown, and yet fear of this happening was given as the major reason for putting barriers in the way of contact. If children are disturbed, and therefore vulnerable to placement breakdown, to add the extra stress of cutting them off from parents they care about, however ambivalently, may make the placement even more vulnerable.

In a study of 1 165 children in care who were placed with permanent new families between 1980 and 1985 (Fratter *et al.* 1991), we found that when other variables were held constant, children who had continued contact after placement with parents, or siblings placed elsewhere, or with other relatives were less likely to experience placement breakdown. In any case it is as well, as Parker points out (1985), to have 'contingency plans', involving a role for the natural parents as continuing concerned adults. If contact has been terminated for some time, or has been allowed to wither, such a role for them becomes much more difficult to achieve. There is no evidence, either, to support the view that contact should be terminated to allow introductions to a new family to be started, and then re-established.

It is usually considered desirable in most cases to place siblings together, or to keep up contact between them if they are placed separately. Berridge and Cleaver's finding of a higher rate of foster-placement breakdown for those placed away from other siblings in care reinforces this view, as does our study of children placed with permanent substitute families (Fratter *et al.*).

The nature of the contact should be decided on an individual basis, depending on the plans for the child's future, and the role which it is intended the birth parents will play. If it is intended that the child should become attached to permanent substitute parents, contact should not be so frequent as to encourage a child to believe that he or she will be returning home to live. It should be frequent enough, however, for the youngster to know the parents well enough to feel reasonably comfortable with them, much as he or she might do with an aunt or uncle who visits from time to time.

The question of the comfort of the people involved – the children, the people caring for them, and the natural parents – is an important one to be borne in mind when decisions about the practical organisation of contact are to be made. It may also be appropriate to vary the nature and amount of contact at different stages in children's lives, and clearly as they get older their own wishes will become more important.

If it is decided that continued contact is necessary in the interests of a child, this should be an important issue when *deciding* about a placement, since no amount of cajoling will persuade substitute parents who are reluctant to allow contact to do so willingly. Their discomfort will become obvious to the child and contact will wither. Much effort has been devoted to discussing the problems of contact and when it should be terminated, but research shows that the bigger problem is in helping and encouraging parents to *maintain* contact in the interests of their children, even when it is painful to them. The publications of the Family Rights Group (1982, 1986) are important sources of practical help in achieving the sort of contact which is helpful to children and comfortable for the adults concerned. The issues around 'open adoption' are more fully explored in the publication on the subject edited by Mullender (1991) and in a video in which the views of the three sides of the 'adoption triangle' are sought (Ryburn 1992).

Case example 1: The Thomas family

Peter Thomas, widower, aged 28, ice-cream salesman
Jean Baxter, divorcee, aged 25
Pat Thomas, aged 6
Jim Baxter, aged 5
Mary Thomas, aged 4
Jenny Baxter, aged 3

Peter Thomas, whose father is Jamaican and mother English, contacts the social services department saying he has left his cohabitee, Jean Baxter, and is living at his parents' house with Pat and Mary. Both Peter's parents work.

He asks for help in caring for his children. The social worker visits him at his parents' home. He is depressed and tearful, and the two girls are anxious and clinging.

Practical problems
His parents are tolerant of his staying there, but do not see this as a permanent arrangement; where will he and the children live? At the moment they are being looked after at various times by Peter's sister, Brenda, either grandparent and Peter. Peter is missing a lot of work and has many debts.

History, problems and strengths
Peter's first marriage ended in divorce. He says his wife was unfaithful to him, and there are hints that this was a violent relationship. Their two children live with their mother; there are large maintenance arrears and Peter is being pressed by the Child Support Agency to make regular contributions. He went to live with, and subsequently married, a widow, also of mixed parentage, the mother of three children. Pat and Mary Thomas were born but their mother became seriously ill. After a painful illness, during which Peter – with support from a family aide – cared for the whole family and nursed his wife, she died when Pat was four and Mary, two. He tried to care for her three children as well as his own two but was unable to do so and her three children were accommodated by the local authority and placed with maternal grandparents. A residence order to the grandparents has since been made. Peter is in contact with the children and he, Pat and Mary are still quite attached to them. There were many debts, including rent arrears, and despite social work and family aide help, Peter decided to give up his home. He moved in with his mother, and the two girls with their auntie, Brenda. After about six months he went to live with Jean Baxter who had just left her husband after many violent incidents. (Jean is white.) Pat and Mary went too. The relationship was stormy but Peter says he still loves Jean and wants to go

back to her. He believes she loves him but that her parents are telling her not to have him back.

Peter says that problems revolved around money and Mary's jealousy and her rejecting behaviour towards Jean – in particular, Mary's habit of making herself sick. However, on further discussion it seems that both Peter and Jean were insecure in the relationship and jealous of each other. Peter finally left after he and Jean had a fight about Jean's previous husband's access to their children, Jim and Jenny. In this first interview, as well as providing the background information, Peter says that he does not think life is worth living if he cannot go back to Jean, and that he took a bottle of pills the night before. He also says he cannot live on his own, and that he is a failure with women.

- How would you respond to Peter's request for help?
- What practical help would you offer?
- What emotional support would you seek to offer?
- What would be the arguments for or against providing accommodation for the children if Peter asks for it? If so, what would be your thoughts about where to place the children?
- What clues do you have about how the needs of the children can best be met?
- What further information do you need to make an assessment of how best to help Peter and the children?

In answering these questions, specify the legal provisions which sanction your actions and discuss the strengths and weakness of the alternative possible actions. Pay particular attention to the reasons for deciding whether the children are 'in need' or 'are suffering or likely to suffer significant harm' and the implications for your work of these decisions.

Case example 2: Jenny Haynes

Jenny Haynes is the youngest of three children. When she was three, her parents separated. All the children stayed with their mother and saw their father infrequently. When Jenny was seven, and her sisters, Emma and Pam, were 12 and 14, their mother died of cancer. The two oldest girls carried most of the burden of nursing their mother and caring for Jenny for the last two months of their mother's illness. The maternal grandmother provided emotional support, but suffered badly from arthritis and could not offer much practical help. Social services became involved just before the mother's death and provided a family aide. The two oldest children promised Mrs Haynes that they would look after Jenny and all stay together.

After the death, Emma and Pam went to stay with an aunt, but she could not have all three children and Mr Haynes, who had remarried and had a baby of two, decided to have Jenny to live with him. Mr Haynes contributed to the keep of the oldest girls. He offered to have them live with him but they did not want to leave their friends and he lived in another town.

Jenny was showing signs of stress towards the end of her mother's life: she was withdrawn at school, started to wet the bed and increasingly told lies. Although apparently wanting to go to live with her dad, and being keen to be with the new half-sister, Mary, her behaviour became more disturbed and she started to become 'spiteful' with Mary. She became cheeky and rebellious with the new Mrs Haynes. After eight months, Mrs Haynes, now pregnant again, said that either Jenny went, or she did.

Mr Haynes contacted social services and requested that Jenny be provided with accommodation on a long-term basis. He said he did not feel his wife would ever come to love Jenny, or that Jenny would ever allow her to get close. He was unsure about his own feelings for Jenny. He had recently lost his job and could no longer afford to contribute towards the keep of Emma and Pam. His solicitor advised

him to ask whether the local authority would pay a residence order allowance if the aunt applied for a Section 8
residence order. Jenny was placed in a 'bridge' foster
home where contact with all members of her family was
encouraged.

   Whilst she was at the foster home, it became clear that:

1   Jenny was attached to her granny and her two older
    sisters with whom she had stayed in contact.
2   Granny and the two older sisters were angry with Mr
    Haynes for letting Jenny go to a foster home.
3   Granny was unable to offer a home to Jenny, though
    she could have her for weekends if Emma or Pam went
    too; they had done this twice whilst Jenny was at her
    dad's.
4   Jenny talked about her dad, and her new mum and sis-
    ter, and said, but without much conviction, that she
    would like to go back. She seemed to repeat her sisters
    'parrot fashion'. She ought to go back to Dad because
    Dad ought to look after her. She also said she would
    quite like to have a new family, especially if they had a
    dog.
5   Mr Haynes did not think he would ever make a home
    for Jenny. He felt sorry for her, but she still felt like a
    stranger to him, and he knew it was either Jenny or his
    new family. He would like to stay in touch with her, but
    would be guided by the social worker about what was
    best. He was rather shocked when the possibility of
    placement for adoption was mentioned, but then said
    he would consent if the social worker thought it was
    best, but would still like to keep in contact 'at Christmas
    and birthdays'.
6   Sisters and Gran are keen on a long-term foster place-
    ment near the sisters (their aunt can't have her
    because she has a child of ten who doesn't get on with
    Jenny). Sisters, the aunt and Gran are vehemently
    opposed to adoption.

Balance the advantages and disadvantages for Jenny of:

1   Placement directly for adoption.
2   A foster placement with a view to adoption.
3   A foster placement with a view to a later application for a residence order.
4   A long-term foster placement.

Would continued contact with her dad, sisters or grandmother, be appropriate in any of these placements?
What legal steps would need to be taken to achieve your desired plan?

5 Achieving permanence by return to the child's natural family

By far the largest proportion of children who go into care or are accommodated (around 90 per cent according to Bullock *et al.* 1993) return at some point to live with parents, or to their home communities.

There can be no doubt that a youngster's need for stability and security, together with his or her need for a sense of personal identity, can best be met by returning permanently to live with both or at least one natural parent, provided that they can provide 'good-enough' care – either alone, or with continued help. In America acceptance of this premise has led the specialist 'permanence' units to develop services in such a way as to offer maximum support to children returning home to their birth parents. However, the research studies already discussed, together with a recently completed study by Farmer and Parker (1991) of children in care who went home 'on trial', indicate that it is the exception rather than the rule for well-planned and adequately resourced services to be offered to such families in Britain, even when the children are technically still in care but living with parents or relatives.

Almost by accident in Britain, workers whose initial role was to prepare children for permanent placement with new families, found that the skills they had developed could be used to help children return to original families. The 1986 brochure of the Barnardo's 'New families in Yorkshire' project states:

We consider that the social work skills needed to reintroduce a child to his or her birth family and ensure the plan succeeds are very similar skills to those involved in "introducing" a child to a new family and supporting the placement. We are keen to extend our work of finding permanent families for children to restoring children to their birth families if this is appropriate. (Barnardo's Yorkshire Division 1986)

Chances of success

Bullock and his colleagues (1993) have summarised the research on outcomes for children who return home from care, and produced helpful check-lists to give guidance about the likelihood of success for placement back home (Dartington Social Research Unit 1992).

In America the Oregon project (Lahti 1982) was able to 'permanently' place 233 of the 259 children who had been assessed as unlikely to return home and for 45 of these (24 per cent) the placement involved return to natural parents. Approximately two years later 80 per cent of these children were still there, a breakdown rate which is about the same as that for 'hard-to-place' children placed with permanent new families in Britain (Wedge and Thoburn 1986, and Fratter *et al.* 1991) but considerably lower than that for 'long-term' foster placements (Berridge and Cleaver 1987).

Stevenson and Smith (1983) found that 23 per cent of 167 children discharged from voluntary care after at least six months, came back into care before the end of the research period. Trent (1989) found that, when properly resourced, placements back home of children in care referred to a voluntary agency for placement with new families, were as successful as placements with substitute parents. On the other hand, Farmer and Parker (1991) found that 43 per cent of the placements of children who had been committed to care and returned home 'on trial' broke down within two or more years of placement. However, using a wider range of outcome measures, they rated 77 per cent of the placements of the 172 children who went into care for reasons of protection, and 81 per cent of the 149 older 'disaffected' children, as 'adequate' or 'positive'. They also note that a relatively small proportion broke down during the first year of the placement, and that even those placements which did not last served the purpose of letting the children re-establish contact with parents and wider family. For some of the older children in particular, this facilitated a move to a more successful placement with relatives. This is an important and detailed study which, with the study by Bullock and his colleagues (1993), identifies variables in the families, the children and the social work process which are associated with successful outcomes. It should be essential reading for social workers responsible for deciding or supervising the placement of a child back home from care.

Using a fairly rigorous definition of 'success', Rowe and her colleagues (1989) found that only 46 per cent of the placements home with parents of children aged nought to four, and 23 per cent for the over-tens, lasted as long as expected and met the desired aims.

An encouraging note in favour of return home as a first option in most cases is the finding of Fein *et al.* (1983, p. 509): from a study of 187 children 'stuck' in the care system, 100 of whom returned home, those for whom rehabilitation was tried settled more successfully, even if they were eventually placed with permanent substitute families.

Lynch and Roberts (1982), in one of the small number of British studies which use objective as well as subjective tests of wellbeing, studied 42 children who had been abused and their 41 siblings, and came to a similar conclusion. They showed that most families whose children returned to them and who were offered a comprehensive service were enabled to offer good enough care to the children and to those born after the abusing incident. This is not to say that the children were unscathed by the abuse, and siblings born after the incident were more likely to be rated as doing better than the abused children being brought up by the same family.

These studies all suggest that there is much room for improvement in practice and resources for children who return home from care, and that, on a more hopeful note, such improvements are associated with more successful outcomes.

Which children and what sort of practice?

My interviews with parents and social workers of children who went home 'on trial' (Thoburn 1980), led me to the conclusion that children returned home not so much as a result of planned decisions by social workers about the best interests of the child, but rather because of the decisions of others – either those caring for them saying they would no longer do so, or the determination of parents and children that they should be reunited. Vernon and Fruin (1986), with a much larger study of 185 children, came to the same conclusion. Farmer and Parker (1985, 1991) found that

> in practice, it appears that the initiative for a child to be allowed home on trial is taken more often than it might appear by the parent or young person. Placement breakdown is another important reason. One local authority had conducted a study of all its children on care orders who were home on trial in 1981 which it kindly shared with us. Of the reasons recorded for the home on trial decision, 'planned rehabilitation' was given in only 40 per cent of the cases. In another 40 per cent of the cases, half were because a placement broke down and half because of changes in the situation of the parent or child or parental pressure. (Farmer and Parker 1985: 9)

Stevenson and Smith (1983) found that many workers were taken by surprise when parents asked to resume care of children who had been in voluntary care for over six months. In studying 339 cases where the provision of Section 56 (Children Act 1975) applied, they found that social services departments implemented sensibly their power to require 28 days notice. However, their finding that 30 per cent of parents had not been informed about the Section, implies either a lack of legal knowledge on the part of the workers or a lack of contact prior to the request. (This administrative mechanism by which local authorities assumed parental responsibility for children who were received into care at the request of their parents was ended by the Children Act 1989.)

Although the involvement of parents, children and care-takers in decisions about discharge from care is to be welcomed, it seems important to consider how the social workers can become more involved in planning for return home, and discharge their obligation to make decisions in such a way as to *promote* the welfare of the child throughout childhood. Farmer and Parker (1991) found that the chances of successful placement back home were increased by social workers who could maintain a clear sense of purpose, together with a readiness to use their authority.

Factors in the children and families which have been associated with successful return home by most of the researchers already cited include:

- the child being under the age of two when placed at home;
- the parents having regular contact with the child whilst he or she was away;
- the parents attending reviews when the child was in care;
- parents being willing to think through and talk to each other and social workers about the problems they may encounter when the child returns;
- no new serious problems in relation to child care emerging whilst the child was in care or during the placement at home;
- the fact there was not a younger step- or half-sibling already in the family when the child returned;
- the child continuing to have a role in the family throughout the care experience; for example, by keeping toys or other belongings at home, and his or her bed or bedroom and personal space being retained.

However, they stress that factors should not be considered on their own, but rather as they contribute to the total picture.

Some questions to be answered

As well as the more general questions outlined in the placement options check-list in Chapter 4, consideration should be given to the following questions if a child may be returning home.

- Does the child want to go home? If, as may well be the case following a prolonged period in care, he or she is unsure, particular attention should be given to the power relationship of the adults discussing this. It may be appropriate to involve a psychologist who is not identified with a particular option and has a different range of techniques for interviewing youngsters.

- Who has parental responsibility for the child and will it be necessary for applications to be made to court for Section 8 orders such as contact or residence orders?
- What is the nature of any attachment between the youngster and each member of the family to which he or she will be returning? Particular attention needs to be paid to new members of the family, such as step-parents, and step- or half-siblings.
- Will assistance be needed to secure comfortable contact arrangements with a non-resident parent if the child is returning only to one parent?
- If attachments are minimal, ambivalent or non-existent, as with a new step-parent, or when a child left home as an infant and has been there for some time, how can attachments be established, re-established or strengthened?'
- Is care likely to be 'good enough' or, as the Children Act puts it, 'what it would be reasonable to expect' a parent to give to him or her? This will depend on the needs of the child as well as the abilities of the parents; a youngster with physical or learning disabilities, for instance, or one who is emotionally or behaviourally disturbed, will need more care than a child of robust and resilient temperament with no particular difficulties.
- If care is unlikely to be 'good enough', can it be made 'good enough'? What help will be needed in order to do so, and what supervision will be needed to check that it remains so?
- Is the youngster likely to test out renewed or new relationships, and in what ways? Most youngsters who have been cared for away from home for some time will do so.
- Are the parents likely to be able to accept and cope with testing out behaviour? What help will they need to enable them to do so, and are they likely to ask for help if the going gets tough some time after the child returns to them?
- Is this a case where care is mainly 'good enough' but may deteriorate at times of stress? Particular attention should be given to this issue with parents who are known to be impulsive, to react aggressively or to have a short temper,

to abuse alcohol or drugs or where there is a recurrent pattern of delinquent behaviour which may lead to imprisonment. Such factors are especially important if the child is to return to a single parent.

- What arrangements can be made in these circumstances to detect signs of stress and help the parents, and provide protection and continuity for the child?
- Do the parents accept the need for such arrangements? Respite care might be one such facility, but is a scheme available which will allow respite care to be offered by the same family, or residential unit, and thus avoid the damaging effects of multiple placements in different homes? Could the previous carers take on this role?
- Is the child on a child protection register? If so, a child protection conference should be convened, to which all those who attended the original conference should be invited as well as those currently working with the family. (See Beckford Report, London Borough of Brent 1985, on this point.)
- What form of agreement between the parents, the youngster (if old enough) and the social workers is appropriate to ensure that a child who may be at risk is adequately protected, and that the parents and child receive appropriate services? The *Placement of Children with Parents Regulations* (Guidance and Regulations, Vol. 3) give details of what an agreement must contain, and the Family Rights Group and National Foster Care Association (1991) have produced suggested agreement forms based on the regulations and the principles of working in partnership.
- Should the same worker offer a relationship to parents and child, or would it be appropriate for a different worker to be involved? It is especially important that if there is any possibility of significant harm to a child, he or she should spend time regularly with a trusted adult. This is even more important with young children and may need the involvement in the agreement of a teacher, health visitor, day care worker, youth worker or family aide or volunteer.
- What will be the source of the family's income? What financial and practical support will be needed to support the placement, and how can this be made available to reduce the risk of practical pressures destabilising the placement?

Questions about legal status

If the child is accommodated, no formal notice is required before parents resume care of a child. However, the agreement with parents should include details of the arrangements for the child to go home, including a period of notice which is appropriate in all the circumstances. The longer the child has been in a particular placement, the more important it will be for enough time for preparations for the move to be made, and goodbyes to the foster carers and friends to be said.

If a care order has been made the child could remain 'in care' but be placed at home under the placement of children with parents regulations. Alternatively – and a route which should be considered more often than it is – the local authority or parent may apply to the court for the discharge of the order after a satisfactory programme of visits home. It may also be appropriate to ask for the care order to be replaced by a supervision order; if necessary with conditions attached, such as a requirement for regular medical checks for the child, or for the parents to regularly attend a family centre or mental health outpatient clinic.

If the return home of the child and the discharge of a care order appear in the child's interest, but a phased return home is desirable – perhaps because they have been out of touch with each other for some time – one possibility is for the care order to be discharged and the child to remain in accommodation during the reintroduction. In other cases a supervision order with conditions allowing for a residential period may be substituted for a care order, the residential period allowing for a gradual return home.

It is important that the decision about placement at home in care, on a supervision or Section 8 order, or no order at all, should be taken on the basis of the child's needs and what is appropriate to the circumstances of the family, rather than as a matter of routine or for purely practical reasons. In my study of children at home 'on trial', I found that social workers preferred to keep a care order in existence in order to obtain material help, a situation also found by Farmer and Parker (1991). If statutory authority is not necessary, support – including financial and practical help – should be made available under Section 17 of the Children Act.

I found in talking to parents and young people, that whilst a minority welcomed the continuation of statutory *supervision,* and most accepted it as necessary, they were usually made extremely anxious by the power of the social worker to remove a youngster without going to court. (This is also an anxiety felt by substitute parents of children placed permanently, either for foster care or for adoption prior to the adoption hearing.) This anxiety, and the split responsibility for the youngster, which may encourage some parents to use the threat of the child going back into care as a disciplinary measure, may undermine the sense of permanence which is as crucial for the stability of a placement back with the family, as it is for placement with new families.

The home 'in care' status has practical disadvantages too. Since the major parental responsibility remains with the local authority and not the parent, social workers should be consulted before a youngster goes on a school holiday or stays with friends or relatives overnight, and such arrangements should be formally approved. Whilst this may be appropriate for young children, and failure to do so has been identified as leading to tragedy for some young children placed at home 'in care', for the majority of older children this provision is likely to cause tension between parents and youngsters and is frequently ignored as a result. Thus an element of deceit may come between the social worker and the parents. The requirement for an annual medical may also be a source of disagreement and tension for older children.

A good agreement which results from the social worker spending time with the child, the carers and the parents and anticipates any events which may require approval, or any stresses which may arise, can help overcome such difficulties. However, the spirit of the Children Act suggests that, wherever possible, the status of home 'in care' should be avoided or last for short periods only to try out the feasibility of return home. Only in exceptional circumstances should it be necessary for longer periods for some children who are seriously at risk of suffering significant harm.

Practice issues

Good practice for rehabilitation starts with admission. A well-prepared admission to care, and an appropriate placement, will make the social worker's task in returning a child home considerably easier, whereas the opposite may make it impossible.

Agreements should detail not only what is expected of the parents and child, but what is expected of the care-givers, social workers and others offering help. They should also make clear what can be done to change the agreement if it proves not to be working well, and how parties to the agreement can complain if others are not fulfilling their part of the bargain. A well-established complaints procedure, together with clear written information about rights and responsibilities (such as that contained in the Guide for parents of children in care produced by Harlow Parents' Aid, or the Family Rights Group and NSPCC Guide 1992), will help increase the power of the families and care-givers vis-à-vis the local authority in what is an inevitably unequal relationship. Opportunities to re-negotiate the agreement and to assess progress occur routinely at the child's review, but in many cases it will be inappropriate to wait for such long periods and any party to the agreement should be able to ask for a further meeting to discuss progress and changes. The Family Rights Group publication (1986) and training material (1991), and the work of Maluccio and his colleagues (1986), give more detailed guidance on working in partnership with parents. The training pack of Lewis *et al.* (1992) gives practical suggestions and exercises to aid working in partnerships when there is an issue of child protection.

Services for families and children need to be carefully planned and agreements made both for the transition stage and for when the youngster returns home.

Relationships

Jenkins and Norman (1972) used the term 'filial deprivation' to characterise the feelings and reactions of parents whose children have been taken into care or accommodated by the local authority. Earlier British writers, notably Winnicott (1970) and Stevenson (1968) have described parents in similar terms.

Although some may seem predominantly angry, whilst others retreat into depression or apathy, underlying these reactions is a severe assault on the self-esteem of people whose sense of their own worth is likely to be already fragile as a result of marriage failure, mental illness or being judged as unable to offer adequate care or control to their children.

Children also tend to blame themselves for the events which led to their leaving home, and this is especially so if they have been abused. Thus both whilst they are separated – and especially when they come together after separation – parents and children are likely to need reinforcement about their worth which can best come from satisfying relationships with those they care about.

It is likely that in many cases self-esteem will need to be boosted by therapeutic or supportive services which offer a caring and consistent relationship with a social worker or other professional, family aide or volunteer. In some areas volunteers, perhaps attached to a Home-start scheme (van der Eyken 1982) or NEWPIN scheme (Gibbons 1992) fulfil such a role. Other families may receive continuing support from parents' aid groups with whom they may have made contact when the youngster left home, especially if they were in dispute with the local authority social worker about the necessity of statutory action (Monaco and Thoburn 1987). Sometimes care-givers are able to play a continuing role in supporting the reunited family, and can be especially helpful if they are able to take a youngster overnight if pressures build up or if respite care is needed (Burch 1986, and Aldgate *et al.*, in preparation).

Some local authority and voluntary organisation family centres provide drop-in facilities so that families may support each other; and group work with children and parents (including fathers) may meet their need for supportive relationships and friendship as well as for therapy. I have referred earlier to the challenge to social work to find an effective model of longer-term help for vulnerable families, which does not create unnecessary dependence. If there has been disagreement between the worker and the parents about whether the child should leave home, or about whether statutory action was necessary, careful thought should be given to whether a different worker should be allocated to either the child or the parents. Usually in the process of working together to get the youngster back home, and to work out a suitable way of helping, a relationship of trust will be formed even if the original reaction of the parents was one of anger and mistrust. However, there is evidence from consumer studies that some parents are unable to trust the worker who removed their child (Thoburn 1980, Millham *et al.* 1986, and Monaco and Thoburn 1987). In these circumstances it is appropriate to allocate a different worker. The same may also apply to the child who, having been removed once, twice or three times by a particular worker, becomes anxious that his or her continued visits will mean removal yet again.

Services

The services already described as being necessary for prevention are equally relevant to rehabilitation, and the importance of viewing supervision as a service and part of a 'protection plan' is especially important for those who return home to families where they have previously been neglected or ill-treated. Marsh and Triseliotis (1993) discuss the organisational and practice issues in greater depth.

The role of financial and material help must also be emphasised, given that children returning home from care may have extra difficulties resulting from separation and reintegration. Such difficulties may include bed-wetting, destructive behaviour and other difficult behaviour which leads to extra costs.

Many children will return home to a reduced standard of living because their families will be dependent on income support (the income support rate for children is approximately a third of that estimated by the National Foster Care Association as being necessary to keep a child of the same age). Discussion of the financial position and the material needs of families of children returning home is an important part of preparation for rehabilitation, and any necessary financial or material help should be included in agreements about return home. The impact of the Child Support Act 1991 on family income may be positive in cases where it leads to a non-resident parent playing a more practical role, but negative if conflict about money increases stress in the family.

Section 17 of the 1989 Act provides for assistance in kind and in exceptional circumstances in cash, and the return home of a child who has been for some considerable period in care should be seen as an exceptional circumstance. Such assistance should be offered in a positive way, rather than, as is so often the case, grudgingly and only if a parent plucks up the courage to ask. I found in my research that parents were very loath to ask for help, since this made them feel even more inadequate, but were extremely heartened when workers checked with them if there were any practical ways in which they could be helped.

The least which should be required is for children leaving care to have adequate beds, bedding, furniture, clothing and shoes. If there are children already living in the family in deprived circumstances, it will be important to minimise jealousy by making efforts to ensure that they, too, are adequately clothed. Liffman (1978), in his book about an Australian family centre, *Power for the Poor*, describes an experimental project which guaranteed for a three-year period a reasonable income to 62 families who had severe problems. In Britain, although many social services departments stress the importance of prevention and rehabilitation, only Strathclyde (Freeman and Montgomery 1988), to my knowledge, has gone on record as systematically attempting to improve the income of deprived families whose children are at risk, if necessary by offering direct financial aid. Other forms of practical help, such as the provision of telephones for single parents so that they may have access to help at times of stress, and payment for baby-sitters, are important ways of helping to reduce stress. Respite care may also be necessary, and should always involve planned arrangements with the same care-givers rather than emergency action. Now that it has been accepted that lack of finances should not prevent children finding permanent homes with new adoptive families, it is no longer tenable to allow placements back home to fail because of lack of practical and financial resources.

Another area in which the service to children returning home from care is likely to differ from that to new families, is in the necessity for monitoring the health of the parents. It is now accepted that people in manual occupations and those in receipt of benefit are more likely to suffer from chronic debilitating health problems. Whilst social workers pay attention to mental health, they have a poor record for spotting physical health problems and helping their clients to obtain appropriate care and treatment (Gibbons *et al*. 1990).

Finally in this section on practical help, I mention the need to help youngsters whose parents may have separated either before or during the care experience to stay in touch with a parent, siblings or other important people from the past. In many cases it is more possible to do this when a youngster is looked after by the local authority than when he or she returns to a parent who may still feel bitterness or anger towards the absent parent and wish to shut him or her out. The skills of mediation and negotiation are essential for workers in such cases; and the availability of comfortable surroundings – away from a child's home, including at weekends – might make the difference between continued contact and loss of a parent figure, brothers and sisters, and other relatives. Some family centres offer an 'access' service, and children's home staff who are developing expertise in helping parents have satisfactory visits to their children in care could extend this service to children at home and non-resident parents.

Words or therapy

The principles for deciding which methods of social work might be most appropriate have been explored in Chapter 3. Given the low self-esteem of most parents whose children have been looked after by the local authority for anything more than respite periods, it is especially important that whichever model of helping is chosen, there is a strong element of partnership, with the maximum amount of power and control given to the parents that is consistent with protecting the youngsters. The process of drawing up an agreement about respective roles when a child returns home, gives the opportunity for the worker to explain to families the alternative methods of helping, and allows them to join in a discussion about what is most acceptable to them. Obviously workers must advise the parents about their own views of the likely benefits of different models of helping, but a method which does not have the parents' support is unlikely to be successful.

Family therapy methods are frequently used, and have many advantages in such situations especially where the placement's success will be dependent on a stepfamily and new step- or half-siblings integrating children returning home as part of the new family. However, the consumer literature indicates that family therapy is not always acceptable to families, and that others would much prefer counselling or other models of service (see especially Howe 1989). Also the requirement to attend a clinic or family centre rather than being offered a service at home may seem unhelpful to some whilst being preferred by others. Family therapy and other brief methods of social work may be appropriate on an episodic basis at times of particular stress, but it may also be necessary to offer a counselling or support service over longer periods.

The skills of working with children and care-givers, which have been developed by workers in specialist permanent placement units, are also appropriate both for the stage of reintroducing youngsters to their birth families, and for subsequently supporting the placement (see Chapter 6).

Managerial issues

> Jim is at risk because of my lack of time. This is really a Family Service Unit case. [His mother] knows I will try to be there if she really needs me. But sometimes she comes down so often, I have to tell her to go away. I'm afraid one of these days I will misjudge it. Also, I am not firm enough with her over Jim. I haven't the time to pick her up consistently. (Thoburn 1980, p. 86)

This comment from the social worker of a youngster placed at home 'in care' gives an idea of the stresses on those who undertake this work. The Beckford Report (London Borough of Brent 1985) explored in some detail the nature of the social workers' involvement and the importance of supervision. A report of the Social Services Inspectorate (1986) commented on the inadequacies of social work supervision in cases where abused children return home from care.

A policy which seeks to reunite children with the parents they care for and wish to be with, must seek to offer a service in those more complex cases where, even with considerable help whilst a child is being looked after, significant problems will remain, especially at times of stress.

A management strategy for maximising the effectiveness of social work with children who are to be offered the advantages of permanence by returning home to natural parents must provide competent, confident, well-supervised and well-supported workers who have time and energy and feel sufficiently secure to work imaginatively and take necessary risks. It must also provide an environment in which parents and children feel both safe and welcome when they ask for help.

In her study of social work with angry parents, Lowe (1987) found that the bureaucratic nature of social work services contributed to the anger felt by many parents. In my two studies of children who returned home, or lived with substitute new parents, I was struck by the similarity of the language used to describe the upsetting effects which insensitively delivered services had upon family life.

The importance of working with new families from small intimate units has been accepted by many local authorities as well as by the voluntary agencies; yet most work with natural families is still undertaken by a generalist worker. If a child care specialist is involved he or she is often working from a busy area team with inadequate consultation, administrative back-up, reception and interviewing facilities and out-of-hours cover.

Maluccio and his colleagues (1986, p. 199), reviewing research on 'permanent placement', found that biological families – rather than adoptive or permanent foster families – had the greatest requirement for services when children returned to them, and stated that 'it may be necessary to acknowledge that some children and families will need after-care for long periods, perhaps for life'. If this seems a somewhat daunting prospect, it should be taken alongside the view of specialist adoption workers that some adoptive families will need continued services, albeit of an episodic nature, until the children reach independence. Jones (1985, p. 143), after studying a range of intensive family services, recommends a long-term approach where

> the intensity can rise and fall based on the needs of the case; the service boundaries are permeable so that families can easily enter and leave and re-enter; and the emphasis of the service programme is upon 'being there', providing continuity, and serving as a resource to the family, rather than upon providing a time-limited, goal-oriented service, and closing the case.

If such a service is to be made available to substitute families, is it not appropriate to offer it also to some natural families taking children home from care? Especially since, as we have already seen, many of them are also new 'reconstituted' families, and the children's problems are often no less serious than those of children moving to substitute families.

Case example: The Thomas family, part 2

After discussion, Peter decided that he did not want to be parted from his daughters and therefore was not requesting accommodation for them. The social worker had several interviews with Jean, Peter and all four children. Jean said she did love Peter, but that she could not cope with Mary's rejecting behaviour. Peter was offered a housing association flat and helped with furniture. A day nursery place was found for Mary, and Jean looked after Pat after school until Peter finished work. In a series of family interviews Peter and Jean started to look at the problems they experienced when living together, and ways of improving the situation. The social worker also started to work directly with Mary, and with Mary and Jean jointly to help to improve their relationship and Mary's behaviour. An agreement was made whereby Peter and Jean would meet weekly with the social worker to try to sort out their difficulties. Peter would not pester Jean to take him back for three months and she would give him a definite answer at the end of that time. Problems to be worked on in order of importance were:

1 Mary's relationship with Jean.
2 Debts and inability to manage financially.
3 Relationship between Jean and Peter, especially their lack of trust in each other.
4 Housing problems.

Jean discovered that she was pregnant. The detailed agreement was a non-starter due to impulsive behaviour by both Peter and Jean. Peter frequently collapsed saying he could not cope on his own. At one stage he insisted on the children being accommodated that evening after taking a combination of drugs and drink. He withdrew the request but the social worker subsequently took him and the children to meet a short-term foster mother because it looked as though placement might be necessary.

After about a month Peter gave up his tenancy and moved back in with Jean. Both said this was what they wanted and for a few weeks things went quite smoothly. The social work service previously agreed was resumed and there were also visits at times of crisis. Mary's behaviour deteriorated. She again started to reject Jean and frequently made herself sick. After a series of minor injuries to Mary, which Jean admitted causing, a child protection conference was held and Mary's name placed on the child protection register. Jean began to say more frequently that she could not love Mary. Discussions took place about whether Mary should go to a foster home, and whether a care order would be applied for.

One morning, about five months later, the worker was called out by Peter saying that Jean had gone mad and was throwing things at the children. She arrived to find broken plant pots on the floor, Jean's neck badly grazed by Peter, supposedly in order to restrain her, and Mary with cornflakes in her hair, Jean having thrown her breakfast at her.

Jean said she no longer felt able to care for the girls, although she did not know how she would feel after the baby was born. She admitted to hitting and biting both of them. Peter said that if he had to choose between the children or Jean, he would have to choose Jean. He therefore asked for the children to be accommodated until after the baby was born, as he thought some of the problems were due to the pregnancy making Jean feel tired and irritable. A child protection conference was held, and Mary's name was placed on the register as being likely to suffer physical and emotional harm.

Jean agreed with the plan for the girls to be accommodated, saying that she really wanted to make a home for them but had not the energy to cope with Mary's difficulties in her advanced state of pregnancy and she thought Mary and Pat ought to stay together. Her own two children would shortly be going to stay with her mother until after the baby was born. It was due in six weeks time.

Pat and Mary (now aged seven and five) and the parents were carefully introduced to short-term foster parents, Mr and Mrs Unwin. They settled well but Mary had difficulties at school, being described as exceptionally clinging, and stealing from other children's lunch boxes.

Both girls were pleased to see Peter, Mary, Jim and Jenny when they visited but were upset when they left. Three months later (a month after brother Paul was born and following a child protection review) the girls went back home.

1 Draft an agreement between the worker, Peter, Jean and Mr and Mrs Unwin for the children to be accommodated, bearing in mind the regulations in the Children Act 1989, guidance Volume 3.
   And/or role play the meeting which draws up the agreement.
2 After consulting *Working Together under the Children Act 1989* (DH 1991d) role play the child protection review conference held before the children went home.
3 Draw up an agreement between those who will be helping ensure that on their return home the children's needs will be adequately met.
   And/or role play such a meeting.

6 Long-term placement with relatives or friends

Chances of success

One of the legacies of the Colwell Report (see especially Olive Stevenson's minority report, DHSS 1974), and the report into the circumstances of the death of Tyra Henry (Lambeth 1987), has been a sense of unease about placements with relatives. Although many children in care are fostered with relatives (27 per cent of the 200 long-term foster children studied by Rowe and her colleagues, 1984), these situations do not fit easily into the literature about foster care practice, and there has been a widespread but unsubstantiated feeling that such placements are not entirely satisfactory. However, Rowe and her colleagues (1984) found that these were amongst the most successful placements studied. In particular they found that the children's 'sense of permanence' was greater than that generally found in non-relative placements, and that the children had a strong sense of their own identity. They were less likely to have had several placements in care, and their wellbeing was likely to be higher. Their relative foster parents were more likely to welcome social work contact, and to find it more helpful and less threatening. A majority maintained contact with at least one natural parent. Nine out of ten were considered by social workers to be providing a good or excellent home for the child. The natural parents were slightly less positive than the foster parents or children about these arrangements, especially if the care-giver came from the other side of the family. Nevertheless there was a tendency for difficult family relationships to improve over time, and mostly

> parents were relieved to have their child kept within the family and many appreciated being able to visit freely. Those who also had children who were being fostered by strangers almost invariably made comparisons in favour of the in-family placement (Rowe *et al.* 1984: 187)

The authors note that the proportion of children in their sample fostered by relatives varied from 44 per cent in one authority to 11 per cent in another.

Since all these placements had lasted for at least four years, this study inevitably leaves out those unsuccessful placements which broke down at an earlier stage. However, Lahti (1982) and Fein *et al.* (1983) found that permanent placements with relatives both in terms of stability and wellbeing were more successful than the other permanence options. Berridge and Cleaver (1987) found that only two of 25 long-term placements with relatives broke down within three years; and in a later study Rowe and her colleagues (1989) found that children placed with relatives tended to be older than those placed with 'stranger' foster parents, but that when this age difference is held constant more of the relative placements had satisfactory outcomes.

These research studies by Rowe and her colleagues, the Colwell Report and a small American study by Liddy (1970) indicate that placement with relatives will not be appropriate if differences between natural parents and the relative foster parents are irreconcilable, leading the two sets of parents to do battle over the child. However, Rowe and her colleagues have indicated that children are able to cope with some disapproval of a natural parent by their relative foster parents, and that relative foster parents are able to see the advantages of encouraging continued contact, even with parents of whom they disapprove. Thus if there seems a possibility of placement with a relative meeting a child's needs, or if a youngster is already living with relatives but there is dispute between the two sets of parents, careful assessment will need to be made not only of present difficulties but of the likelihood of them being resolved with time. The skills of conciliation and mediation (Parkinson 1986) are particularly appropriate in helping workers to make such an assessment. Family group meetings of all those involved may be appropriate, and there is growing interest in such meetings following the strong emphasis in the Children Act on seeking the views of family members. Ryburn (1992) suggests how family meetings (which are part of the legal child protection system in New Zealand) may be adapted to the UK situation.

Legal issues

In considering placement with relatives or friends as a long-term option, several legal routes are now available. Children may live with relatives with the agreement of the parents, or a Section 8 residence order may be sought; or they may be discharged from care and placed with relatives or friends either by the parents themselves or by the social worker in partnership with the parents and relatives. When appropriate such placements can be supported by Section 17 provisions, including cash or a residence order allowance; or the child may be accommodated or in care and placed with the relatives as a foster child. The choice will depend on whether the parents take direct responsibility for the placement or whether it is arranged by the local authority or an order made by the court, as well as on the financial circumstances of the relatives, and any perceived risk to the child, which requires more formal supervision.

As with placements of children in care with parents, it is desirable in most cases for the care order to be discharged as soon as possible. Should social work support or therapy be appropriate, this should normally be made available under the provisions of Section 17 and Schedule 2 of the Children Act 1989, since it is important that it is clear that power and responsibility lie with the relatives. This may be particularly important if a youngster has had several moves whilst being looked after by the local authority, since social work involvement may well make him or her anxious about another move. Discharge of the care order before placement may also diminish the tendency for relatives caring for the child to use the threat of calling in the social worker to move the child as a means of enforcing good behaviour (reported by Rowe and her colleagues 1984, and Maluccio and his colleagues 1986). If this arrangement proves viable, it can be given legal recognition quite quickly by an application for a residence order with the parents' consent, or after three years if the parents do not consent.

If the child is placed from care to a relative, and there is concern about the level of care even though this is the best available placement, a supervision order may be appropriate. Residence orders can be tailored to suit individual circumstances by the addition of contact orders, specific issues orders, prohibited steps orders or court injunctions.

Residence orders are likely to be especially attractive to youngsters who resent the interference in their lives which comes from being looked after by the local authority, notably the necessity for reviews, medicals, social work visits and other minor or major annoyances. (Teenagers, who are looked after by the local authority and living with relatives, find it particularly annoying that the social worker's permission has to be gained if they wish to stay with friends or other family members.) Those children or relatives who are anxious about removal by the local authority or the natural parents will also be reassured if a residence order, which conveys parental responsibility, is made. Lowe (1991) provides a helpful overview of the legal position of grandparents following the Children Act; and the Grandparents' Federation is a source of detailed advice and support.

The adoption law review consultative document (DH 1992) discusses adoption by relatives; in general it considers that it will rarely be appropriate.

There is no study as yet of children's attitudes towards residence orders. In our interviews with older children in permanent substitute family placements, we discussed this issue and found that the majority were interested in a legal status which would transfer the power to make decisions in their lives from the local authority to the people actually caring for them. Although none of these were relative placements, there is no reason to believe that children placed with relatives would feel differently. Bullard *et al.* (1990) found that custodianship was just beginning to gain in popularity with relatives before it was abolished by the 1989 Act and replaced by the residence order. Some of the children they interviewed considered it very appropriate to their circumstances.

Residence orders do not allow a youngster's name to be changed legally without the permission of the parents or the court, but this is rarely a problem with relative placements – as it may be with placements with strangers – since the name is often the same anyway. Many older children make decisions to be known by the name of the people caring for them even without parental permission. Once they reach the age of 18, of course, parental consent to change a name by deed poll is no longer necessary. Alternatively names can be changed by making a declaration to a solicitor.

Perhaps the reason why custodianship, the previous legal status, found little favour amongst foster parents, whether relatives or strangers, was that placements were rarely made with this in mind, and substitute families have grown used to the foster care status, or have planned from the start to seek adoption. In making new placements, following the Children Act, workers will be able to discuss the advantages of residence orders alongside those of the other placement options. There are already indications that more children are being placed with relatives as an alternative to being committed to care (DH 1993).

On the other hand, a residence order may not help with other problems reported by children and relatives who are foster parents. Where it is in a youngster's interest to know that he or she will remain for the foreseeable future with relatives – though the parents find this hard to accept, and seek every opportunity to challenge the placement – long-term foster care, with the continued role of the social worker as intermediary, or adoption will be more appropriate, depending on the circumstances.

Practice issues and support to the relatives and the child

The nature of the social work service will vary considerably, in some cases having much in common with social work with children being looked after on a permanent basis by substitute new families, and in other cases having more in common with social work with natural families. It is important to stress that mediation and negotiation skills may be especially important in offering a service to relatives or friends caring for children. It is as important for such children to have the opportunity of maintaining contact with the parent who is not related to the care-givers, as it is for step-children to have the opportunity of remaining in contact with a non-resident parent. It will often be helpful for special facilities to be available, such as access centres which allow a parent to feel at ease with his or her children when visits to the relatives' home are uncomfortable and it is not appropriate for the youngster to go to the home of the parent.

The question of financial support to a placement with relatives is an important one, and lack of finance should not be allowed to prevent the success of an appropriate placement. Foster care has often been used in the past simply to support a relative foster family financially, particularly in cases where there would be disagreement between the natural family and the foster family over money, thus causing dissent which could damage the youngster and threaten the security of the placement.

The Child Support Agency will in future be involved in helping to secure maintenance from both parents if they have the means to contribute. Experience of matrimonial disputes about custody of children shows that finance is often at the root of such disputes. Natural parents may willingly enter into an agreement to pay regular contributions to the relatives, and these may be topped up by a residence order allowance. On the other hand it will not be appropriate for the relatives to be dependent on spasmodic contributions from the natural parent which may be a source of friction. It is not as yet clear how sensitive the Child Support Agency will be in such circumstances, and what degree of flexibility there will be in the respective roles of the local authority and Child Support Agency.

Case example: Emma and Pam Haynes

Look at the case history of Jenny Haynes at the end of Chapter 4. At the stage when Mr Haynes asked for Emma and Pam to be accommodated, what would be the advantages and disadvantages of:

1   A local authority accommodation placement with their maternal aunt (a single parent with a three-year-old daughter) as foster parent?
2   Supporting the father's placement of the girls with their aunt by supplementing child benefit and a small contribution made by their father with Section 17 1989 Children Act money?
3   Short-term accommodation and placement with the aunt and encouraging her to apply for a residence order?
4   Supporting the arrangement as in number 2, with encouragement to apply for a residence order?
5   What would your recommendation be about a residence order allowance, and how would this affect, or be affected by, an assessment for child support made by the Child Support Agency?
6   Draft (or role play, the drawing up of) an agreement between all those involved in ensuring that the placement will meet the children's needs.

7 Permanent placement with substitute families

Until recently social workers wishing to place a youngster with a new family, with the intention that the parents should become the 'psychological' parents of the child, had to decide whether to seek the assistance of the adoption section or the fostering section of their department. (This is still the case in many authorities.) A detailed study of permanent family placement over the last 15 years brings me to the conclusion that such a distinction impedes the chances of successful placement for many children who are unable to return to their original families.

Initial assessment, or an unsuccessful attempt to return a child home, may indicate the need for placement with a substitute parent or parents who will commit themselves at least until he or she reaches independence. At that stage a full assessment of a youngster's needs, along the lines discussed in Chapter 4, will clarify which of the permanence options is likely to be most appropriate. Such an assessment will also clarify the child's needs in terms of continued contact or otherwise with members of the birth family and other important people from the past. All too often decisions about contact are influenced not so much by the needs and wishes of the youngster, or even the original family, but by the wishes of the new parents who have been approved and are waiting for a child to be placed with them. Indeed many social workers are so convinced either that no family will be found who will encourage contact or that continued contact is likely to increase the risk of placement breakdown, that they make little effort to seek new families who are willing to help children to keep in touch with important people from the past. If a youngster is already in a placement which is intended to be permanent and attached to new parents, their views about continued contact will become a significant factor in the decision. Hence the advantage of 'bridge' placements which can allow a proper assessment of needs, and the search for an appropriate placement which can accommodate those needs.

Which route to permanence for which child?

A worker seeking permanent family placement for a child now has a choice of three legal options: adoption, application for a residence order and foster placement (see Figure 3, page 63). In a study of 1 165 children placed permanently by British voluntary agencies between 1980 and 1984, before the residence order became an additional option (Fratter *et al.* 1991), we found that 58 per cent had been adopted between 18 months and 6 years later when the survey instrument was completed, 61 per cent were fostered with a view to adoption and 14 per cent permanently fostered. Twenty per cent (including 16 per cent of those who had been adopted) had continued contact with parents, siblings or other close relatives. Within these broad bands, placements may be made in different ways. For example, a youngster may be placed directly for adoption under adoption agency regulations; as a foster child for a brief period with the intention of moving to adoption within a period of months; or as a foster child with a view to adoption, if this subsequently seems to be the appropriate course of action, but with no definite time-scale in mind.

This wide range of placement choices should not be an excuse for indecision. It provides the opportunity to move from the rather crude equation of permanence with adoption noted by the Short Committee (House of Commons 1984), to the possibility of meeting the need for permanent placement of a wider range of children. We have already seen that over 60 per cent of children in care in 1989 were over the age of ten. Of the 167 children aged under six on admission to care studied by Millham and his colleagues (1986) – those who might most easily fit into adoptive families – only 25 were still in care living away from home or relatives two years later, and thus possible candidates for permanent family placement of one sort or another. With the proviso that the needs of each child must be individually assessed, with special consideration given to sibling groups in terms of individual needs versus the need to be placed together, I offer guidance about the different placement options which might be appropriate for different groups of children.

Adoption

Despite case material which indicates that a small proportion of adopted children have extreme difficulty in coming to terms with their adopted status (see especially Howe 1992), all large-scale studies of the wellbeing of adopted adults conclude that this is a generally successful means of meeting the needs of those children unable to grow up in their own families. Though 'success' rates vary and different measures of 'success' are used, the average 'satisfaction' rate is around 80 per cent, and this applies to those adopted beyond infancy (Kadushin 1970, and Triseliotis and Russell 1984) as well as to those adopted as infants (Raynor 1980, and Thoburn 1992a).

These studies give me confidence in supporting the view that adoption should be the placement of choice for all those children whose parents request it, and where there has never been a significant relationship between the youngster and the natural parents. Most children in these categories will be babies or toddlers. However, they will include older children (even teenagers), being looked after by the local authority, who have lost touch with members of their birth family, or who see no value in continuing a relationship with them, and express consistently and over a prolonged period a wish to become full members of a new family.

One of the most encouraging findings of recent research (Macaskill 1985, Thoburn *et al.* 1986, and Wedge and Thoburn 1986) is that adopters *can* be found for children with physical and mental disabilities. Such placements, especially of babies and toddlers, have a very good chance of meeting the needs of the youngsters for love and security as well as their physical needs for remedial help. They also appear to bring joy and a sense of achievement to the new parents, to compensate for the hard work involved in caring for a multiply handicapped child.

The question marks over adoption concern both feasibility and desirability. Our recent study of children placed by voluntary organisations found that as children get older the chances of successful placement for adoption diminish; those who have a history of deprivation or abuse, those who are institutionalised, and those who have emotional and behaviour problems are at greatest risk of disruption. The disruption rate 18 months or more after placement was 13 per cent for those placed before their ninth birthday and 37 per cent for those aged nine or over at placement. In a more detailed study (Thoburn *et al.* 1986) we found that youngsters who had had good enough care from a parent figure in the past seemed to be more able to cope with separation and to make a new attachment than did those who had been ambivalently attached to parent figures in the past. The latter group included many of those who had been abused or neglected, and whose capacity to trust had been severely impaired. Older children who have learning difficulties also seem to be particularly likely to have problems in settling with new families (Wedge and Thoburn 1986).

Prior to the Children Act 1975 adoption was only possible in Britain with the consent of the natural parents, except in very limited circumstances. It is only in the last 15 years or so, as the placement of older children for adoption has increased, that courts have been more willing to dispense with parental consent. A note of caution must therefore be introduced, since we do not as yet have any large-scale studies of the wellbeing of adults placed for adoption as older children against the wishes of parents who they were fond of or concerned about. Morris (1984) also warns of the dangers of placing children for adoption against the wishes of the children themselves, and indeed Fitzgerald (1983) notes that a child's ambivalence about the severance of links with the original family was often associated with placement breakdown. We found in our study of children referred for adoption by the Children's Society (Thoburn *et al.* 1986, and Thoburn 1990) that enthusiastic social workers sometimes did not listen hard enough to what youngsters were telling them about the need to stay in contact with members of their birth families. Our study of 1 165 children placed with permanent new families showed that whilst social workers considered continued contact with natural parents to be desirable for 20 per cent of the children, only 15 per cent of those still in placement two years later retained contact (Fratter *et al.* 1991).

Although there may well be circumstances when placement for adoption against the wishes of the birth parents is appropriate, great care should be exercised in such cases, and the older the child, the more risky will such a placement be.

Adoption with contact, sometimes referred to as 'open' adoption or 'contact' adoption, should be considered in such cases. Careful consideration will need to be given to the nature of contact both at the time of placement and in future years. The willingness or otherwise of the first parents to accept that their child will remain permanently with a new family and become attached to them as parents, will be a very significant factor in making such a decision, as will the temperament of the natural parents and thus their ability to play a role which meets the needs of the child. However, the timing of the decision about whether they *can* play this changed role is crucial. Few parents who are opposed to placement are able to talk about what they will feel and do *after* placement, until they are convinced that there is no chance of their child returning to them. This usually means that the work to consider their role in the child's life can not really start until a clear decision has been conveyed to them by the court that an application for the child to return to them will not be successful. Under the Children Act 1989 a judge can make this clear by stating that no further application for discharge of the order will be accepted without leave of the court, and that the court is unlikely to give such leave. It is therefore necessary in many cases to have a period of time between the decision about legal status and long-term plans and the decision about contact once the child has been placed, to allow this work with the parents to be undertaken. The *Adoption Law Review* (DH 1992) strongly suggests that a social worker other than the child's worker should be available to work with them if they are not in agreement with the plan for placement.

If a youngster is already attached to carers who are to become the permanent substitute parents, then the temperament and wishes of that family must also be carefully considered. There may be less scope for flexibility about parental contact than if a new family is to be chosen with the specific needs of the child in

mind. The Barnardo's 'Cambridge cottage project' (Fratter *et al.*
1982) has undertaken pioneering work from a residential base in
assessing the needs of the child before looking for the placement,
and has shown that if children are assessed as needing an adoptive placement with continued family contact, such placements
can be found and can be as successful as other placements. The
Barnardo's Colchester team undertakes similar work using
'bridge' foster carers in this way (Westacott 1988). The importance of making every effort to allow the child to have some
form of contact with members of the birth family after adoption
is underlined by our finding from the adoption survey previously referred to (Fratter *et al.* 1991), that such contact appeared to
be a protective factor in that it was associated with the placements lasting. Mullender (1991) has edited a collection of papers
on open adoption, and Ryburn's video (1992) gives the views of
parents, children and adopters.

When the placement for adoption of black children or those of
mixed parentage is being considered, special care must be taken
to meet their needs for a continued sense of racial and cultural
identity. Since the British Adoption Project demonstrated in the
early 1960s that black children were not, as had been previously
thought, 'unadoptable', black infants have not been considered
'hard-to-place' since white families are available as adopters if
no same-race placement can be found. However, recent research
findings indicate that adoption of black children by white parents, whilst adequately meeting most of their needs, rarely
enables them to grow up with a pride in their racial and cultural
identity or, as adults, to cope with racism (Gill and Jackson 1982,
and Ahmed *et al.* 1986). As a result African, Caribbean, Asian
and other babies from minority ethnic groups, and black children of mixed parentage, are once more considered to have special needs when it comes to placement for adoption. Agencies
including the Independent Adoption Society and several
London boroughs developed new ways of recruiting black and
Asian adopters, which have been taken up by other agencies, so
that it is now comparatively rare for black children to be placed
with white adopters. The research on the placement of black
children is reviewed in the Appendix to the Adoption Law
Review (DH 1992).

A worker of different race to that of the child he or she is seeking to place for adoption, should have access to advice and information from a member of the child's community. The search for a family of the same race who can also meet the youngster's other needs may take longer, and therefore the 'bridge' placement becomes even more important. Although babies should be placed as early as possible, there is reason to be hopeful that they will settle in with a suitable new family if care is taken over the introductory period. My own conclusion is that provided that good care can be offered in this way, it is preferable – even for babies – for a same-race placement to be made, even after some delay, than for a more rapid trans-racial placement. Weise (1987), writing from the perspective of a black social worker, concludes that it is babies – even more than older children – who need a same-race placement, since older children will already have established a black identity before leaving their first families. While they too should be placed with families of the same race, religion and culture wherever possible, their other needs may become more important, and it may be possible to find other ways of keeping their already established sense of identity, in particular by making sure that they remain in contact with their original parents or relatives. Particular care is needed in choosing a placement for a black child of mixed parentage who has been brought up by a single white parent, or lived for some time with white carers. Maximé (1986), Small (1986), and Banks (1992) give helpful advice on the work needed to help such children to feel comfortable with themselves and their racial inheritance. The importance of such work is emphasised by the finding that black children of mixed parentage (most of whom have in the past been placed in white families) were more likely to experience placement breakdown (Charles *et al.* 1992).

'Secure' foster care

Most of the problems surrounding foster care as a permanent placement come from its ambiguous legal and administrative position embodied in law and the regulations. Despite the fact that many children have over the years grown up in foster care which they and their foster families have seen as permanent, foster care in Britain is legally defined and managed as if it were only temporary. The Children Act 1975 went some way to recognising the long-term commitment many foster parents and children make to each other. It attempted to resolve the difficulties, however, not by offering a greater sense of security to foster families as such, but by making it more possible for foster children to be discharged from care to the full custody of their foster parents either through adoption or custodianship (a legal status which no longer exists and has been replaced by the Section 8 residence orders).

Long-term foster care is usually seen as the least desirable alternative, and this is understandable in view of the higher breakdown rates in some earlier studies compared with adoption. Berridge and Cleaver (1987) found that 36 per cent of 188 planned long-term foster placements with strangers made by two local authorities broke down within three years. Rowe *et al.* (1989) found that 22 per cent of the 345 long-term placements ending during the study did not last as long as needed, and 10 per cent lasted too long. However, the latter authors note that two-thirds of the long-term placements were rated as successful and 'those that did last were evidently highly regarded' (p. 114).

One problem is that even with *planned* long-term placements (and the foster placement agreements required by Children Act regulations should ensure that all involved are clear about when a placement is intended to be permanent), a sense of *insecurity* may be created by the behaviour of the social worker supervising the placement, and the way in which reviews and medicals are carried out. Some authorities delegate only minor decisions to the foster parents, and disapprove of signs that show a child is becoming a part of the new family, such as a request from a youngster to be allowed to use the new family's surname. Recently examples have been brought to the attention of the National Foster Care Association of insensitive handling of allegations of abuse made against foster parents. Other foster carers hear of these incidents and are made to feel insecure by them. Clearly allegations of abuse made against substitute parents must be investigated, but it is important that agencies reach agreement with their foster carers about how best to handle these investigations to minimise the risk of unnecessary placement breakdown.

Administrative practice can undermine, and indeed has undermined, the sense of security and permanence of foster children and foster families; we do not know how successful long-term fostering might be if a 'sense of permanence' were encouraged. Interviews with children and their foster parents carried out by Rowe and her colleagues (1984) and in our study of permanent family placement (Thoburn *et al*. 1986) suggest that they feel more anxiety about *social workers* removing the youngsters than about natural parents doing so.

Fostering with a view to adoption

Fostering with a view to adoption has also to some extent fallen into disrepute, but findings from America (Lahti 1982, and Fein *et al*. 1983) suggest that, like fostering with relatives, it should be resurrected as a placement of choice for some children. Lahti found that wellbeing scores were higher for those adopted by foster parents than those adopted by strangers. It is important to stress, though, that a short-term placement should only be confirmed as a 'permanent' placement after a new home study focusing on the different role of permanent parents has been undertaken by a different worker, and the change agreed by the adoption or permanence panel.

It is important to remove administrative and practice obstacles to a sense of permanence in long-term foster care since there are significant numbers, especially of older children (albeit smaller than in the past now that the residence order is available and open adoption is more acceptable), where 'permanent' foster care will be the placement of choice. Also many children will live as foster children for months or years before being adopted and a sense of permanence at the early stages of the placement can be crucial to success.

It has long been assumed that the majority of long-term foster parents wished to adopt their foster children, and that the majority of long-term foster children would wish to be adopted if offered the opportunity. This view contributed to the provisions in the Children Act 1975 which gave more security to foster parents applying to adopt. However, the numbers who did so were smaller than expected and Rowe and her colleagues tease out some of the reasons why some foster parents wish to adopt and others do not. Only 37 per cent of the long-term foster parents who adopted said that they always wanted to adopt, and the most frequently cited reasons were that 'this particular child was very special to us' (84 per cent); 'we wanted to end the insecurity' (83 per cent); 'the child needed the security' (83 per cent); and 'we wanted to be fully responsible for this child' (70 per cent) (Rowe *et al*. 1984: 200).

Some foster parents who would have liked to adopt were prevented from doing so for financial reasons, but this should no longer be a reason for children remaining in foster care with the availability of adoption allowances and residence order allowances. Rowe and her colleagues had more difficulty identifying why some foster parents did *not* apply to adopt. They did find that the behaviour of the foster children was more disturbed than of those who were adopted, with foster parents valuing the help of the social services departments in dealing with these behaviour difficulties. Other than that, they concluded that 'the decision to adopt a child, like a decision to marry, is personal and intimate, and inherently unlikely to be susceptible to measurement and statistical analysis' (Rowe *et al*. 1984: 205). (The need for social work support should not be seen as an obstacle to adoption or application for a residence order since in such cases the child would be a child 'in need' as defined by Section 17 of the Children Act, and the new parents are thus entitled to a supportive service irrespective of legal status.)

It is not therefore easy to offer a list of the sorts of children for whom secure fostering with a permanent new family will be a placement of choice. There will be those older children who, when all alternatives are explained to them, will make an informed choice of foster care as most likely to meet their needs to remain in contact with people from the past but also to have a secure and loving family life. They may well not wish to take the enormous step implied by adoption but a residence order may still leave them feeling vulnerable. This will particularly be the case with those whose parents have given them affection in the past, but who suffer from personality or mental health problems which might lead to impulsive behaviour and threats to the security of the placement. In such cases the local authority's role as intermediary between the two sets of parents offers greater security to the placement, and is valued by the children and the foster parents.

Permanent foster care may also be the placement of choice for some very disturbed youngsters, or those with very severe physical or learning disabilities, especially in the case of older children. In such cases the foster parents will value the availability of social services department support, and shared responsibility. With children who present very severe problems, new parents may be willing to commit themselves throughout their own lifetime, but hesitate to commit their children and relatives to continued care of such a youngster.

If a child is already attached to a foster family and it is decided that the placement should be confirmed as permanent, and attempts to rehabilitate cease, there may be reasons particular to that family which mean that neither adoption nor a residence order, even with payments, are appropriate. Rowe and her colleagues have shown that many placements originally intended to be short-term become long-term, and warn that 'social workers will need to beware of having preconceived ideas about what foster parents will want or should want' (Rowe *et al.* 1984: 205). In the enthusiasm for adoption there have been examples of social workers pushing foster parents to adopt when they are reluctant to do so and creating in them feelings of guilt or disaffection.

Alongside children who are originally placed in short-term foster homes which become permanent placements, there will be others placed as foster children with the intention of moving towards adoption or an application for a residence order, but where it never quite seems the right thing to do. Several of the families in our study of permanent family placement (Thoburn 1990) intended originally to adopt, but although they remained committed to providing a home for the youngsters for as long as they needed it, they did not come to feel that adoption was appropriate.

Residence orders

As far as new families are concerned, the residence order is intended to provide a status somewhere between that of adoption and foster care, although it may also be used as a short-term measure pending a court decision. It is likely to be particularly useful in those cases where it is inappropriate for links with the past to be legally severed in the full sense of adoption, and as with long-term foster care it is more likely to be the placement of choice for older rather than younger children. It will be particularly appropriate for children living permanently with relatives.

The biggest advantage of the residence order over foster care is that it gets rid of the annoyance and insecurity which the status of being in care engenders in some foster children and their new parents or relatives. It is particularly appropriate when natural parents and new parents get on well with each other.

The corollary is that in those cases where continued parental contact is in a child's interests, but the two sets of parents feel antagonistic towards or suspicious of each other, the application for a residence order may be inappropriate in that it removes the right of either set of parents or the child to *insist* on the authority playing a conciliatory or intermediary role. We have already noted that such help could be available under the provisions of Section 17 of the Children Act, but there may well be anxiety that children not in care or formal accommodation will be given a lower priority. Another disadvantage in some circumstances is that it normally ends at the age of 16 though there can be exceptions to this. The Adoption Law Review Group is suggesting that it should be possible to add a condition to the order which conveys on the new parents or relatives the status of '*inter vivos* guardian'. This would increase the sense of permanence and security of all members of the new family.

Despite the lukewarm reception given to custodianship (the forerunner of the residence order) by foster parents who had either grown used to being foster parents or wished to move towards adoption, it had advantages to offer many of the older children who resent the restrictions which are associated with being looked after by the authority. It is therefore important that the possibility of an application for a residence order be discussed with children as well as with those who are caring for them, and that this should be on the agenda for reviews of all children for whom it could possibly be appropriate. It will be most used in future when, after assessing a youngster's needs, placements will be made 'with a view to an application for a residence order' as they are currently made 'with a view to adoption'. There are indications that some black families will find this a more appropriate status than either adoption or long-term foster care, and that more families will come forward who have considered long-term foster care in the past but rejected it because they fear being hurt if a youngster leaves them.

The residence order allowance will be important to such families. However, the interrelationships between the Child Support

Agency and any assessments it may have made in respect of natural parents, and the local authority and the residence order allowance, need to be ascertained. The local authority has more flexibility in decisions about charges, and, in the light of parental circumstances, often decides not to pursue claims for maintenance of children being looked after. The Child Support Agency may not have this flexibility, and there could be circumstances when the making of a residence order to a new parent or relative in receipt of income maintenance might lead to conflict as a result of sudden demand for a not inconsiderable weekly maintenance assessment.

Legal issues

In discussing the advantages and disadvantages of the different forms of permanent substitute family placement, I have already covered many of the legal issues. However, it is important to remember that decisions about adoption or residence orders are ultimately decisions for a court, and this is an area in which members of the judiciary tend to hold strong views. In the past, some judges expressed a dislike of adoption with contact, preferring custodianship if continued contact with natural parents or with siblings placed elsewhere was considered to be in the interests of a child. While this may often be the case, there will be occasions when adoption *is* appropriate, even though contact is difficult if not impossible to enforce once an adoption order has been made. The duty placed on the Social Services Department by Section 34 of the Children Act to 'allow the child reasonable contact with his parents; any guardian of his' or a person in respect of whom a residence order was in force, has led to important changes and has significant implications for adoption practice.

A Section 8 contact order may be attached to an adoption or residence order, and indeed can be applied for with leave of the court even after an adoption order is made. Problems of enforcement remain, however, and it is generally agreed that it will rarely be appropriate to interfere to this extent with the way in which adopters carry out their parental responsibilities.

However, the requirement to work towards establishing comfortable contact arrangements for children looked after by the authority will mean that plans for adoption will more frequently be made when children and parents still have meaningful relationships. It will be illogical if, having worked hard to achieve comfortable contact, the authority then cuts it off or severely curtails the frequency simply in order to place the child for adoption. The tendency of agencies to look for permanent placements which can facilitate contact will be reinforced by the requirement in the Children Act (Section 22, 4) that authorities must ascertain the wishes and feelings of parents and other important adults, and the child, before taking decisions, and must give them due consideration. When asked their views about contact a large proportion of parents and children ask for it to continue after placement.

In the first year after the implementation of the Act, there were a number of applications for contact orders by parents whose children had been in care for some time, and where contact had previously been terminated in order to facilitate an adoption placement. Some of these were successful and Lord Butler Sloss in an important judgement reported in *The Times Law Report* (31. 12. 92), made it clear that, irrespective of previous decisions of courts or local authority plans, the court being asked to sanction refusal of contact must give paramount consideration to the child's welfare, and must 'not make the order or any of the orders unless it considers that doing so would be better for the child than making no order at all' (Section 1, 5).

Although it is desirable for contact arrangements to be agreed between the two sets of parents prior to the placement, and adjusted as the child's needs change, it is possible even after adoption for any person to seek the leave of the court to apply for a contact order. This is most likely to be used by parents, relatives and, perhaps especially, siblings, if a voluntary agreement entered into by adopters is not adhered to. It sometimes happens that when siblings are placed with separate families but promised that there will be ongoing contact, one or other of the new sets of parents refuses to let this continue. In such cases the adopters may help the other child to seek leave to apply for a contact order or an older child may do so in his or her own right.

Change of name

An issue which has symbolic as well as legal and practice implications is that of change of name. Children joining permanent new families often wish to be known by the surname of the family and this, alongside the wish to be rid of social workers 'interfering in their lives', is an important reason given by older children I have interviewed as to why they wished to be adopted.

Social workers placing children with permanent foster families, or with a view to adoption, should discuss with parents and children the advantages and disadvantages of this and help them to make their own decisions about which surname to use, and whether the new parents are to be referred to as Mum and Dad. With the permission of all those with parental responsibility, or of the courts, children may change their names formally through other procedures than adoption, such as making a declaration that they wish to be known by a new name, or by deed poll.

Natural families are often resistant to their children taking the name of the new family, and for this reason it may often be appropriate to dissuade a youngster from taking this step. However, the views of older youngsters, especially if they are strongly expressed over a period of time, should take precedence.

If such a *de facto* change is decided upon, social workers can help by encouraging doctors, dentists, teachers and others to use the new name and make note on their records accordingly. Some of the older children we interviewed told us that one of the things which made them most angry with local authority workers was the fact they refused to acknowledge their decision to use the new family's name when writing to or about them.

A further reason given by some long-term carers for wishing to adopt the child is so that a testamentary guardian can be appointed. This is not necessarily the best way of proceeding, but the anxieties of some permanent foster carers, or those with residence orders, about what will happen if they should die before the child becomes independent, is a real one which should be discussed carefully.

Practice issues

The principles for practice outlined in Chapter 3 apply whatever the placement. However, social work practice with children placed with substitute families is governed by more detailed regulations than is often the case, the principal ones being the Adoption Agencies' Regulations (1983), and the guidance and regulations accompanying the Children Act, especially Volume 3 covering agreements and reviews. I shall therefore pick out here a few pointers to good practice with children and those who care for or about them at the time of the decision about placement, and during the time before the parents and children become committed to staying together as a family, a period which may take a few weeks or several years. I have already referred in Chapter 3 to the supervision role which is necessary for children in care even when no other social work service is needed.

Work with birth families
Work with the original parents of children living permanently with new families will often be similar to work with parents whose children return home, especially as there will often be other children still at home. However, there is the extra dimension that, at least initially, many will oppose the placement of their children with substitute families. This is increasingly likely to be the case as decisions about permanent placement are made at an earlier stage in a youngster's care career, and before the parents are convinced that they are unable to make a home for the child. Some will be angry, others guilty, others depressed and empty, but whatever the reaction contact with them will engender similar feelings of discomfort, guilt, anger and pain in the worker. I consider that wherever possible the child's worker should also be in contact with the natural parents, at least to discuss details of the youngster's future placement, contact and legal status, and to feed back to the small number of children who no longer have face-to-face contact, a realistic picture of how things are for the family.

However, discussions with natural parents whose children are in long-term care and reading the views of members of parents' groups (Monaco and Thoburn 1987, and Prosser 1992) convince me that some parents will not allow themselves to trust the worker who removed their child. Also the requirement for the child's worker to place the welfare of the youngster above all other considerations will sometimes mean that he or she is unable to offer the sort of supportive and caring service needed by some parents, if they are to recover from the grief and suffering of the often cataclysmic events which led to their children needing to be placed with substitute parents. It may be that support and caring may only be acceptable from a parents' group or volunteer, but the Adoption Agencies' Regulations and the *Principles and Practice in Regulation and Guidance* make clear that the adoption agency, or local authority, must offer a full counselling service to parents separated from their children or ensure that it is offered by another agency. This must include discussing with them the various alternatives to adoption; the sort of family with whom the child should be placed; arrangements for contact; and the legal process. At the moment the question of whether the child should be freed for adoption should be discussed with them, but this procedure is unlikely to continue when adoption law is revised.

Perhaps the most painful and difficult area of work is with parents whose children are to be removed at birth because of the high risks involved. Moore (1986, 1992) gives helpful practical guidance about understanding and working with parents who have seriously harmed their children.

Social work with the children

Relationships   The field or residential worker, or the caregiver who has been most involved in helping a youngster reach the decision to move to a permanent new family, is likely to have a close but complex relationship with that child. The stresses and risks are vividly described by one of the local authority workers we interviewed:

> I must say one can get quite hysterical about finding families. My colleagues started making remarks about my being too involved, which I think is quite dotty because how do you work hard at something unless you are committed? So easily these children can be left to drift. They don't drive you, so you have got to create a sense of drivenness from somewhere. In a funny way I don't find him a par-

ticularly attractive boy. But you don't work with somebody's history without getting very close. (Thoburn *et al.* 1986: 147)

During the research we noted especially the stresses and potential conflicts between the different workers at the time when a new family is being chosen and during the introductory period. We concluded that time to undertake the work carefully was essential to successful placement, and particularly time to talk through any concerns or misunderstandings, together with careful recording and communication verbally and in writing, and efficient but friendly back-up facilities. Without this, there is a risk that conflict between workers can affect their relationships with the child, creating a sense of insecurity and anxiety at a time when trust and confidence are most needed.

The other delicate task for the child's worker is to hand over her relationship with the youngster to the new parents in a way which empowers them to take over the caring and helping roles, while sensitively dealing with a youngster's feelings of loss as the worker pulls back to a less significant position. In our study we found considerable denial on the part of new parents, children, and residential and fieldworkers themselves, of the significance of the relationship between worker and child built up over the preparation stage. Workers seemed to fall into the trap of either attempting to continue to be as involved with the child as they previously were – thus risking 'de-skilling' or alienating the new parents as they attempted to take on the parenting roles – or alternatively withdrawing abruptly, leaving a youngster with unresolved feelings of loss. A careful process of disengagement is necessary in the majority of cases if the parents and the child are to grow together as a new family, and the parents to feel confident in their own parenting and problem-solving abilities.

In handing over the caring and helping roles, it is important for the worker to hand over as much as possible of the power which the child will be aware is so much a part of their relationship – the power to find new families, but also the power to remove them from previous homes which so many have experienced since they left home. At this stage the worker must take every opportunity to demonstrate that the new family and older children themselves will play the major parts in taking future decisions. Thus if a teacher phones and asks the social worker to come to school to discuss some aspect of the child's education, it will usually be appropriate to suggest that the discussion ought to be between the new parents, the child and the teacher, and to tell the parents and child that that is what has been done.

Services During the introductory stage, the child's worker will have a major part to play in negotiating the practical details of a child's life with the family. It is often only at the stage of discussing practicalities that it becomes obvious that some placements are not going to work, and introductions have to be terminated. Practical help will, however, normally be arranged through the new parents, rather than directly between the worker and the young person. In particular, once introductory visits have confirmed that the placement should go ahead, it is important for the worker not to take on a negotiating role for the child with the parents. If such a role is still needed there must still be serious doubts about whether the child should move in.

I have already mentioned that a 'checking-up' or supervisory role is necessary when children are still in care; looking out for signs that all is not well, and especially that there is no risk of abuse. Abused children have a tendency to provoke new parents to abuse them yet again.

In the early stages a particularly important aspect of the service provided by the social worker will be to arrange the reviews and make sure that the placement agreement is still appropriate. Children who have had several moves, or are anxious about impulsive or abusive behaviour by their original parents, will be particularly keen to know that they will not be moved on yet again. Older children can be given a copy of the agreement, and their right to seek legal advice and how they might do so should be discussed with them. The Department of Health provides free copies of an excellent booklet on the Children Act written for young people by the staff of the Children's Legal Centre (1992). This is especially important when a child is accommodated, and the child's sense of permanence with the new family may be impaired by the knowledge that full parental responsibility remains with the original parents. In such circumstances the child or young person will need to know the details of the agreed contingency plan for safeguarding the placement, and should have emergency telephone numbers. It may be helpful for the new parents and young person to role play how they would react if the original parents were to attempt to insist on the child returning home against their wishes.

Therapy and problem-solving   Many of the techniques for working with children referred to in Chapter 3 were developed specifically by specialist workers helping children move to new families. Such techniques continue to be of value once a young-ster is placed, and perhaps during times of stress for months or years into the placement. However, careful thought needs to be given in each case to whether the child's original worker, the family placement worker responsible for supporting the family or the new parents should undertake such work. It may often be appropriate to bring in a different agency such as a family cen-tre, family guidance unit or post-adoption centre, which is less identified with a youngster's previous moves and therefore less likely to create anxiety about disruption. There is also room with older children for formal group work, and for self-help groups similar to those facilitated by the National Association for Young People in Care. However, since youngsters joining permanent new families often vehemently reject the 'in-care' image, it may be appropriate for such groups to be specifically for children in adoptive or permanent foster families.

The needs of the 'home-grown' children of the new family should also be acknowledged and some agencies have set up support groups to allow them to talk through the positives and negatives of sharing their parents with children who join their families through fostering or adoption. The Natural Children's Support Group has produced a video, training notes and a book-let for the 'Children who foster' (available from BAAF).

Social work with new families

Relationships   Empowerment is the key to social work prac-tice with new families – from the moment that a decision is taken that a family is likely to be able to meet the child's needs. If one social worker has been involved in preparing the family for placement and another in working with the child, it will usually be appropriate for the major role to be taken by the family's worker. This model is advocated by the majority of the specialist permanent placement units, and is welcomed by families and children alike. The children we interviewed for our study, especially those who had spent many years in care, told us with great relief how much they valued the fact that the social worker visiting was the *family's* social worker and not *their* social worker. This was a point which was also made by the natural children of the new families, who seemed to welcome the idea of a friendly presence who took as much interest in them as in the children placed with them. In *Permanence in Child Care* we describe the nature of the social worker's relationship with the new parents in terms of consultation.

> The parents wanted and for the most part, received, the sort of service which a social worker asks of a team leader. They accepted the workers' ultimate authority but had confidence that the authority delegated to them as parents would not be interfered with unless this was necessary in the interest of the child. Reassured by this they wanted regular opportunities to discuss their activities, explain their difficulties, explore their ideas for alternative ways of handling them, consider other suggestions and receive offers of help in any joint work to be done. They wanted to share their happy moments and successes, receive praise, and share pleasure. For this to happen they needed to feel valued and for all members of the family to be cared about. Finally, they needed to know that in a crisis competent help would be speedily available to them. (Thoburn *et al.* 1986: 170)

It was particularly important for workers to be aware that the new parents perceived them as very powerful people, able to walk in and remove the children almost at whim, and thus to be very careful to be consistent and not to overreact if families talked about difficulties. Any sign of overreaction or the giving of ill-thought-out advice which did not take on board a particular family's way of doing things, led to families being reluctant to share their difficulties.

Substitute parents tend to turn for everyday support either to family and friends, or, as is well documented by O'Hara (1986), to other adoptive or foster families rather than to social workers.

Practical help and services   The major form of practical help needed by new families was in obtaining resources to meet the special needs of the children. This was most obviously the case with children with a physical or severe learning disability but also applied to those with other educational difficulties. Help with the 'statementing' process will often be necessary, so that children's special educational needs can be met. Many agencies now pay a settling-in grant to help with initial expenses if a child is to be placed directly for adoption, and similar grants can be made available to children in foster care. The advantages of adoption and residence order allowances need to be carefully considered. (See Chapter 6 for a discussion of some of the possible difficulties in the overlap between a residence order and child support payments which must not be allowed to get in the way of contact arrangements by souring the relationship between the original and new parents.)

A study of American children in permanent family placement (Nelson 1985) noted that the services most needed by adoptive families of children with special needs were financial help and respite care, including residential care or boarding education. We found that in the early days of placement families were reluctant to accept respite care provided by the authority. However, as time went by and children's problems continued to wear families down when their initial enthusiasm was no longer there to carry them through, the possibility of 'time out' for parents and children become important.

Supervision   Even the most placid and well-adjusted families can sometimes be turned upside-down by the destructive behaviour of some youngsters now being placed with permanent new families, and it is not unusual for family members to lash out, emotionally if not physically. The way in which the worker intends to fulfil the supervisory obligation should be carefully discussed with families, who usually fully accept the need for this. Within the requirements of the regulations, social workers need to discuss with the carers and older children a style of practice for checking on health and wellbeing, and ensuring that children are involved in an appropriate way in the review process, which does not impede the development of a sense of permanence for children or new parents.

As with the children, new parents will need to be clear about contingency plans to ensure the stability of the placement when children are accommodated. The agreement will need to be regularly updated and particular attention must be paid to contingency plans in case original parents ask for the child to return to them. Copies of the agreement, including the contingency plans, could perhaps be reinforced by a letter from the director of social services to be shown to the police or duty social worker explaining why the permanent placement was considered to be necessary to secure the child's long-term welfare, and why an unplanned move was likely to lead to significant harm to the child. The new parents might find it helpful to role play what they would do if the original parents insisted on taking the child home with them. I have discussed this in more detail in an article in *Adoption and Fostering* (Thoburn 1991b) and the legal position has already been discussed earlier in this chapter.

Therapy and problem-solving   In the early stages of placement, the 'sounding-board' model of social work which I have described is most likely to be valued by parents. However, as time goes by, some parents may well need therapeutic services; this may be long after the child has been placed, and often after an adoption order has been made.

Sometimes it is hard for parents to admit to the worker who has placed so much trust in them that they are experiencing difficulties, and in such cases they may prefer to go for help to a different agency such as a family centre.

Cognitive, behavioural or family therapy techniques are often appropriate since they concentrate on the behaviour or interactions causing difficulties in the here and now. If such techniques have been used in the home study phase of work, families will return to them with some confidence. However, some families we interviewed resented the use of family therapy, especially if careful preparation work was not undertaken and they were left feeling that this model of work implied that there was something faulty about their particular family which had caused them to let down the child.

If permanent family placement is to be achieved for more children in care, then risks will be taken and some placements will disrupt (21 per cent of those in our study placed by the voluntary agencies, Fratter *et al.* 1991). If the worker detects signs that this may be happening, the assessment process outlined in Chapter 4 will start again. It will often be appropriate to try a temporary separation before concluding that relationships have irrevocably broken down, and respite care or boarding education may sometimes be appropriate. Sellick (1992) and Aldgate and Bradley (1993) describe how short-term carers can provide respite care for each other or for substitute parents at times of stress. Utting (Social Services Inspectorate 1991) lists this as one of the roles which, in some cases, can be fulfilled by residential care.

It may be that the child's worker is still sufficiently involved and is the appropriate person to resume accountability. On the other hand, if the decision to look for a permanent new family has been carefully taken, and especially if a previous attempt at rehabilitation has been made and proved unsuccessful, it is likely that youngsters whose placements disrupt will already have 'thrown in their lot' with the new family. They are likely to want to retain a connection with them or with the area, especially if they are now too old to move to another family. The majority of pre-adolescent children placed by specialist units whose placements have disrupted have been placed satisfactorily elsewhere. Sixty-seven per cent of the 254 children in our survey who had previously experienced the breakdown of a placement which was intended to be permanent were satisfactorily placed (Fratter *et al.* 1991).

Case example: Jenny Haynes, part 3

Jenny is still accommodated by the local authority. She was not placed with her aunt and moved to a foster home 'with a view to adoption'. Her father agreed as he was promised that he and other family members would still have face-to-face contact with her. She seemed to settle quite well, and still enjoyed contact with her sisters and granny, but after ten months the foster parents said she was very cold with them, her bed-wetting was worse, she told lies and they did not feel that they would ever get close to her.

She was now eight and a half and, with her father's agreement, was moved to another long-term foster home, with the intention as on the previous occasion that it would be a permanent placement. She has now been there for two years. Dad visits occasionally, but she never goes to his house. She sees her sisters and granny quite often as they live quite close. She has settled fairly well and her foster parents would like her to stay permanently. They could be persuaded to adopt her if the social worker really thought that was the right thing. However, they are a bit dubious about adoption because while they are very fond of her, she doesn't really feel 'like one of the family'. Also they know that her sisters and gran are very opposed to the idea; then, too, the fostering allowance is useful as the foster father has just been made redundant. Mr Haynes sometimes says he would agree to adoption, especially as the fact he has to contribute to Jenny's maintenance causes trouble with his wife. However, at other times he goes along with Jenny's granny and sisters, saying that when she is older the family will find a way of making a home for Jenny.

Jenny has been wary of the social worker since her last move, as she had not wanted to leave her last foster home. She also gets upset at being 'different' from her friends, having to have forms for school journeys signed by the senior social worker and having to have medicals. She thinks she would like to be adopted, because that would mean the social worker couldn't take her away. She's not sure whether she wants to change her name. She knows her sisters and gran wouldn't like it if she did, but it would be nice not to have to explain when she goes to her new school why she has a different name from her mum and dad and foster brother.

1   Make out a case for:
    (a) Jenny remaining with her present foster parents as a long-term foster child. How would you seek to increase Jenny's 'sense of permanence'?

(b) The foster parents making an application for a residence order. What would you advise them about an application to the Child Support Agency, and what is your agency's policy about this and the payment of residence order allowances? What contact arrangements, if any, would you recommend to the court, and would you see a contact order as being appropriate, or any other Section 8 order?

(c) The foster parents applying to adopt Jenny. Would you recommend that there should be continued contact with either Mr Haynes, the granny or the sisters and aunt? Would any of the Section 8 orders (including contact orders) be appropriate? What process does your agency use for deciding about adoption allowances, and would you recommend payment of such an allowance in this case?

(d) Placement for adoption with a new family. Would continued contact with any member of the birth family be appropriate? What about Section 8 orders or an adoption allowance?

2 Draft an agreement with the main participants at the time that Jenny first moved to her current foster home. Include details about the social work service to be offered, contingency plans and arrangements for changing the agreement. (Refer to Volume 3 of the Regulations and Guidance and to the suggested agreement forms provided by the Family Rights Group and National Foster Care Association 1991.)

8 Long-term residential care and specialist fostering

I have already considered in earlier chapters the assessment, short-term treatment and respite care roles of residential care and of foster care. In this chapter I consider the roles of specialist fostering and long-term residential care in meeting the 'permanency' needs of those children for whom permanent substitute parents are not appropriate. The two are included in the same chapter, since in most respects they are interchangeable in terms of the children whose needs they may meet. In many other respects they are similar, and this has been increasingly recognised by those recently researching or discussing practice in residential care (especially White 1979, and Berridge 1985).

The Barclay Report (National Institute for Social Work (NISW) 1982) defines residential care as:

> places – including private family homes (usually called foster homes) – where clients live instead of in their own homes, for shorter or longer periods and under a variety of temporary or intermittent arrangements (e.g. full-time, weekdays only, weekends only); these, together with places where clients live permanently, are the 'residential services'. (NISW 1982: 83)

The Utting Report, Social Services Inspectorate, 1991 concludes that the role of residential care is:

to provide 'a home for children who:

- have decided that they do not wish to be fostered;

- have had bad experiences of foster care;
- have been so abused within the family that another family placement is inappropriate;
- are from the same family and cannot otherwise be kept together;

[and to provide] expert, multidisciplinary help with social and personal problems in a residential setting; containment and help in conditions of security'. (SSI 1991: 8)

Residential care exemplifies the growing 'mixed economy' in
social work, especially insofar as long-term care is concerned.
The private or voluntary sector has always played an important
part in the provision of residential child care and education for
children with special needs, and is usually the preferred choice
for the education of children from privileged backgrounds; for
some who have special needs because of a particular disability;
and for some who live in rural areas and need to travel so their
educational needs can be met.

Although my experience of working in a market-oriented system in Canada leads me to view the growth of competition
rather than cooperation with some concern, the issue is compli-
cated by the fact that foster care is a form of private practice in
that specialist foster parents are usually self-employed. Also
small voluntary or private children's homes have long provided
an alternative, not only for some children whom the state sector
has failed but also for many skilled and dedicated members of
staff who concluded that their ability to help children was inhib-
ited by the bureaucratic and play-safe practices of many local
authorities. Sellick (1992) takes up this theme when discussing
the support needs of carers. In her review of the part currently
played by residential units in the provision of long-term care,
Potter (1986, p. 31) concludes that the present range should continue and be expanded to provide a spectrum of choice ranging
from the larger foster homes currently operating at the boundary
of residential care and fostering, to the larger therapeutic units
and boarding-schools.

Studies of specialist fostering (Cooper 1978, Yelloly 1979,
Hazel 1981, Shaw and Hipgrave 1983, and DHSS 1984a) indicate
that there are many similarities between long-term residential
care and specialist foster care. As with residential care, the range
of specialist foster placements is broad. At the one end there is

little distinction to be made between them and short- or long-term 'traditional' foster homes; at the other end of the spectrum, 'professional' foster homes have more in common with thera-peutic residential units. From a study of the specialist fostering scheme in Essex, Banks and Grizzell (DHSS 1984a) concluded that community parenting – rather than foster parenting – would be a more appropriate term. South Glamorgan refers to those caring for adolescents as part of specialist schemes as communi-ty carers, omitting the term 'parenting' completely (Barry 1987). Banks and Grizzell concluded that the specialist foster homes they studied had more in common with residential homes than with foster homes and should be viewed managerially as part of the residential sector.

> Some happily worked nearer to a traditional foster parent role and felt comfortable in this. But the majority saw themselves choosing specialist fostering as a specific form of employment, and sought fuller recognition of their growing expertise in working with dis-turbed adolescents. (DHSS 1984a: 6–7)

They concluded that:

> the scheme needs to be lifted out of the fostering model and to be given a firmer place within the range of services for adolescents, including access to medical, psychological and psychiatric services. This would bring foster parents into the 24-hour per day support system, whilst also enabling them to contribute their expertise to facilities set up locally for the adolescent … the notion of 'community parenting' commends itself to us. (*Ibid.*)

A Barnardo's specialist fostering scheme in the West Midlands combines professionalism with permanence. The scheme aims to provide family-style care for as long as they need it to young people with severe behaviour or emotional problems, including some young people leaving secure units. The scheme recruits, trains, pays and supports carers in similar ways to the earlier professional foster care schemes, except that it encourages the carers and young people to form lasting relationships, and hopes that the young person will remain with the family after leaving care. The provisions in the Children Act for the continued sup-port of young people who have been looked after by the authori-ty until they reach the age of 21, provide a more secure basis for such placements. This project has been particularly successful in recruiting carers who are black or Asian (Caesar *et al*. 1993).

Which children?

Several writers have helpfully commented on the needs of children who may benefit from long-term residential care, as opposed to those who remain there because a more appropriate place is not available. Davis (1981) classifies residential units in terms of whether they are 'family-substitute', 'family-supplement' or 'family-alternative', and Berridge (1985), in a study of 20 children's homes – excluding assessment centres and community homes with education – (CHEs) – found that they were caring for four separate groups of children with very different needs.

Berridge's first group was identified as a transitory group of children, about 10 per cent of the population but involving larger numbers of children because of the way in which they passed through care either to return home or to move on elsewhere. (I have already referred to this use of residential care when discussing the importance of 'bridge' and assessment placements.) He concluded that although not forming a large proportion of the population, they demanded considerable staff time as they were frequently distressed and disoriented when they moved in, and then needed considerable help to move on.

The second group identified, comprising almost half of the children living in homes, were those who had been in care for some period of time – often with previous family placement breakdowns – who were awaiting long-term placements. This group included young children as well as teenagers, and overlapped with the first.

The third group, approximately a fifth of the children but presenting the most intractable problems, consisted of those who had been looked after by local authorities for most of their lives. They were rarely placed with siblings and most had lost contact with their natural families. Most had experienced at least two disrupted foster or adoptive placements.

The fourth group constituted approximately a quarter of the

children. They were young people admitted to care during adolescence, often following family disruption and often having difficulty establishing or maintaining their place in stepfamilies, with whom they nonetheless maintained close contact. Such children are described vividly by Fisher and his colleagues (1986) and also by Stein and Carey (1986) in their account of young people's perceptions of leaving care.

Berridge concluded that these groups had clearly identifiable needs, requiring different care regimes, but that most children's homes sheltered a mixture of children and were thus unable to meet those different needs. This problem has been made worse by home closures, but must be addressed if residential care is to meet the needs of those children for whom it is an appropriate long-term placement, mainly those in the last two groups.

Rowe and her colleagues (1989) note that despite home closures a large proportion of children looked after by local authorities spend some time in residential care, though this is usually for short periods.

The studies of specialist foster care schemes indicate that they are serving a very similar population, including all four groups identified by Berridge, but the flexibility allowed by the smaller groupings means that it is more possible for them to cater for identified groups, and to offer a regime which more readily fits the needs of the children placed there. However, those designing these schemes tend to underestimate the numbers in Berridge's 'long in care' group. All schemes also report difficulties if they impose time-limits (usually approximately two years); youngsters in such cases have lost touch with their birth families, become attached to the carers and need to remain with them until they are able to set up homes of their own (Shaw and Hipgrave 1983). Stein and Carey have pointed out that the majority of these youngsters – especially those who have been in care all their lives, but also some who are using care as a route to independence – are not ready to cope on their own at the age of 18, much less at 16 or 17 when many youngsters are being placed in bed-sit accommodation.

More recently Cliffe and Berridge (1991), in monitoring the impact of the closure of residential homes in Warwickshire, have examined in detail the small group of children whose needs could not be met by foster care or other community alternatives.

To summarise, the children for whom this sort of long-term placement will be needed will be:

1   Those who don't need a substitute new family, since their natural family continues to play an important part in their lives, providing them with the sense of being loved and valued, but not able to meet other important needs.
2   Those who do not want substitute parents, including older children who have been so hurt by previous experiences of living in families, including physical and sexual abuse or previous disrupted placements, and are unwilling to try again; and those making new relationships with youngsters of their own age and turning towards setting up their own families.
3   Those, including quite young children, who need substitute parents, but who have been so damaged by early experiences that they are unable to cope with the closeness of family life.

Which type of placement?

Parent-supplement placements
The preferences of the parents for either foster or residential care will be especially important if care is to fulfil the first purpose, that of providing supplementary care to that provided by the family. Since a major aim here is to help a youngster eventually to move back home or on to independence whilst retaining the support and love of the natural family, the placement which is most likely to further this aim should be the one chosen. There is some evidence (see, for example, Aldgate 1980, and the views of many young people themselves quoted by Stein and Carey and in the 'Who Cares?' literature) that many families and children feel more comfortable about maintaining contact in a residential than a foster placement, although many specialist foster parents are developing skills in communicating with natural parents and conciliating between parents and children.

Residential units or foster homes providing supplementary care will offer a range of regimes. Some, such as Mill Grove children's home (White 1979) and the residential 'families' established by the Children's Family Trust (Cairns 1984), take quite young children, even including those under school age, for periods of years, and are very successful in keeping them in touch with members of their birth families. They thus cater for the overlap between all three groups of children previously listed.

These placements tend to have quite low breakdown rates. Thus, provided that members of the natural family are willing and able to go on demonstrating their love and concern for a youngster, such units may meet other needs, especially the need for continuity, consistency and stimulating experiences.

They provide a particularly appropriate resource for youngsters, including sibling groups, who are ambivalently attached to their parents – perhaps because of emotional or physical abuse, or inconsistent handling in their early years – but whose parents are prevented from offering consistent long-term parenting. For example, their parents may suffer from a physical or mental disability or from an intermittent but severe psychiatric illness, such as schizophrenia; they may be abusers of drugs or alcohol, perhaps on an intermittent basis; or they may be single parents whose delinquent acts lead to periods of imprisonment.

Although the role is that of parent-supplement, for young children such units are called upon to play an important caring and parent-substitute role as well, without totally squeezing out the natural parents or causing the youngsters to feel discomfort as a result of divided loyalties. It should be said that at one end of the continuum, they offer what is very close to a permanent substitute family which enables its youngsters to keep in touch with members of their birth families. Therapeutic units such as the youth treatment centres (see especially Balbernie 1972, Collins and Bruce 1984, Hogughi 1978, and Rose 1990), and, for younger children, the Mulberry Bush school (Docker-Drysdale 1968) and some boarding-schools, may also play this role. Regrettably the high cost of the care and treatment needed by these very troubled children has led to closures as the squeeze on local government budgets has made it more difficult for fees to be met. Placements in such units have also decreased since the revelations about abuse under the guise of 'treatment' (behavioural work in the 'pindown' scandal in Staffordshire and 'regression therapy' in the Leicestershire homes managed by Beck) have led to ill-informed criticism of these therapeutic methods.

Parent-substitute or parent-alternative placements

Most frequently residential or 'professional' foster placements offering 'parent-substitute' or 'parent-alternative' care do so for older youngsters. They will tend to be of three overlapping types. Some offer therapy, usually to the youngsters themselves but possibly also to the family. Bettelheim's work (1955) at the Orthogenic school shows how long-term residential care can meet the needs of some very damaged children for treatment, love and security, and Keith White welcomes back ex-residents of Mill Grove long after they are adults.

The second broad grouping used to be known as 'family group homes'. While these have fallen out of favour in recent years, small children's homes based on a long-term parenting model may still be appropriate parent-substitute resources, especially for sibling groups, and especially if they are encouraged to welcome young people back after they have left care. The third type of longer-term home concentrates on the preparation of older children for independence, a role more likely to be played by local authority units. Although residential units tend to lean in one direction or another, most will offer both treatment and preparation for independence.

The Ockenden Venture and the Save the Children Fund have maintained the value of keeping refugee children together in residential care, thus placing cultural and racial identity at a higher level in the hierarchy of need than is usually the case. Social workers whose caseloads include black or Asian children may learn much from the experiences of these organisations when deciding whether a long-term residential placement might be appropriate.

When careful assessment indicates that a parent-substitute placement is needed, the youngsters themselves should have a major role in deciding whether residential care, or care in a specialist foster home where the regime is not based on traditional family lines, will be most appropriate. Such youngsters are likely to be older, and will be made up mainly of those in Berridge's third group who have spent a lifetime in care, including a majority who have had disrupted family placements. They will also include a small number of youngsters entering care for the first time as adolescents who have been severely damaged by family life, perhaps as a result of sexual abuse, and wish to cut themselves off from their birth families or who have been cut off by them, but do not feel safe in a close family atmosphere.

Unfortunately it is rare for such youngsters to be offered the security of knowing they will stay in one place for a long enough period to form attachments – not only of a non-parental nature with caring adults, but also with the other youngsters and with the local community. Although preparation for independence is important, the greater needs are likely to be for help in such areas as making relationships, learning about themselves as individuals, learning to love and value themselves and to come to terms with past experiences. Such tasks cannot be accomplished if youngsters are not assured of a length of time in which to develop trust in the adults caring for them.

Stein and Carey (1986) point out the dangers of the move by local authorities towards independence regimes.

> The dominant 'independence' message of 'managing on your own' and 'coping by yourself' subtly negates the significance of *inter-dependence*, that is, young people giving as well as taking, getting on with other people and negotiating reality with the support of agencies, neighbours, friends and partners; the very important inter-personal and relationship skills that our young people needed all the time, and which they often found so difficult. (Stein and Carey 1986: 158–59)

The authors characterise some local authority units as offering

> a domestic combat course; young people being marked out of ten on a checklist for each activity, from opening a tin of baked beans to folding sheets, and then 'passing out' when they have reached the required standard. Also in some of the schemes there is a high degree of built-in movement; for example, the young person's preparation may consist of three or four phases of ten weeks each in different units, and if the person 'fails' at any stage he or she may have to leave the scheme or may even be refused council accommodation at the end of the training. (*Ibid.*, pp. 157–58)

These authors point out, as do many specialist foster parents, that young people in this group are often not ready for independent living at 18, let alone at 16 when preparation for independence tends to become the dominant philosophy in many local authority units. They urge local authorities to use all their powers to support youngsters who request it, after the age of 18. The

Children Act allows for the possibility of some residential units and specialist foster homes providing a home for some youngsters beyond their 18th birthday, or to welcome them back at times of distress. Mann (1984), describing the subsequent lives of children who were once on her child care caseload, notes that some residential workers have always welcomed their children back, though this has tended to be disapproved of, and certainly not facilitated, by the care authority.

Foster parents often talk of the costs incurred as they continue to care about and sometimes care for youngsters who have grown up with them; often paying for their weddings and acting as surrogate grandparents. In their need to continue to place new children in specialist foster homes, local authorities tend to be insufficiently helpful when foster parents feel it appropriate to continue playing such a role with youngsters who have moved on from them but may periodically need their support. The guidance accompanying the Children Act on services for young people leaving care or accommodation (Volume 3) is an excellent source of practical advice about how to support young people or those who care about them. All young people and their carers should be given detailed written and verbal advice about services on which they may call. Particular care must be exercised in giving this information to children who have sensory, or learning, disabilities in the most appropriate way.

Perhaps the most distressing group who need long-term residential provision are those who really need substitute parenting, but are unable to accept it. These are likely to be younger children, or those with immature personalities, and they may themselves be asking for substitute family care, but be unable to cope with it when placements are made. Consequently assessing whether such children should be offered long-term residential care, or care in a specialist foster home which does not have as an expectation the idea that they will become part of a new family, is extremely difficult.

Homes for such children need to be long-term – giving them the reassurance that they will not be moved on until they are ready for it – with therapeutic elements as well as a strong caring element which does not replicate traditional nuclear family parent-child relationships. However, some younger children may be helped to such an extent that they are able to move on to a placement with their own or substitute parents.

Chances of successful placement

It is especially difficult to estimate likely 'success' of long-term residential or professional foster care placements, partly because those being so placed are likely to be those whose problems are most severe, and partly because it is unusual for placements to be made which are intended to be long-term. Millham and his colleagues (1986) suggest that in general residential care has a lower breakdown rate than foster care, and the experience of Mill Grove and the Children's Family Trust, already referred to, indicates that when long-term group care is allowed to be long-term breakdown rate can be as low as 8 per cent within five years (Cairns 1984). Rowe and her colleagues (1989) rated 46 per cent of the 1859 placements in residential care in their study as successful and 16 per cent as unsuccessful. On the narrower definition, only 13 per cent of residential placements failed to last as long as needed for those under 11 at placements, and 22 per cent for those over 11. This compares well with the 20 per cent and 38 per cent for foster placements.

On the other hand, Rutter and his colleagues (1983) found that the parenting abilities of 81 mothers who as children had spent lengthy periods in residential care, were lower than those of a group of mothers living in similar circumstances. Triseliotis and Russell (1984) found that 55 per cent of 40 young adults brought up mainly in residential care were 'positive' or 'fairly positive' about the experience, compared with 82 per cent of 44 adopted adults. It seems likely that the quality of residential care is more varied than the quality of adoptive care or placement with relatives or foster placements, and more variable rates of satisfaction are therefore to be expected. Colton (1989) compared the care experience of young people in residential care and foster care, and concluded that the foster carers were more child-oriented than the residential workers and gave the young people more individual attention. Recent enquiry reports have exposed the risk of abuse by residential carers, but, sadly, no type of placement is immune from this risk.

Professional fostering is also difficult to evaluate as it is rarely seen as a long-term option offering 'permanence'. However, it is clear from reports that many 'professional' foster parents continue to offer support even after the youngsters have officially left them. Hazel (1981) considered that for 70 per cent of placements of difficult teenagers the positive aspects outweighed the negative. Early findings from a study of the Barnardo's Midlands scheme of long-term 'professional' foster family care are encouraging (Caesar *et al.* 1993).

Legal issues

Because of the wide range of children using these options, their legal status will be equally varied and need to be considered in each case. It is inappropriate to insist, as do some authorities, that all children using a specialist foster scheme should be in care on a care order. Such a policy may alienate parents and children, especially if a parent-supplement placement is needed, making it more difficult to establish cooperative relationships.

A care order may impose a rigidity which is inappropriate with adolescents as they move into independent living. If it appears that a placement may be disrupted by inappropriate removal from care by the parents, it is possible to protect the placement by applying for an emergency protection order. Young people aged 16 or over can make their own decision to remain accommodated by the local authority. Of course, some children and young people are detained in residential accommodation, including secure accommodation, as a result of offending behaviour. This group – and the provisions of the Criminal Justice Act 1990 – are beyond the scope of this book. Bullock and his colleagues (1993) consider the care careers of some of these young people. It seems more appropriate to resort to the use of an emergency protection order occasionally, if a child is likely to be significantly harmed by removal from a placement, than to start all placements on the assumption that parents and children cannot be trusted to keep to agreements.

In recent years young people in residential care have been offered greater protection by the requirement in the Children Act for the appointment of independent visitors, as well as improved complaints procedures and an improved system for consultation with the young person during the planning and review process.

Practice issues

For children in this group, especially those for whom therapy is appropriate, the helping role is likely to be shared between the care-givers and the fieldworker. Written agreements are particularly important and may be worked out in one meeting with everyone present, or a series of meetings if there are confidential issues which a youngster would not wish to be discussed before other parties. Agreements should cover the aims of the placement and the proposed means of achieving them; including the sort of regime, use of sanctions and contact with parents. Youngsters who have been in a foster home for some time may be reluctant to have personal details about their education, boyfriends or sexual behaviour discussed in front of parents. Parents may be reluctant to discuss certain details about their family functioning in front of foster parents. Foster parents may be reluctant to discuss financial matters in front of natural parents which may be necessary to sort out special payments. Whilst such splitting is to be avoided, it may sometimes be necessary to go along with the wishes of parents, children or carers.

It is important to avoid rigid allocation of roles, such as the fieldworker always works with the parents, and the carer always with the child. Sometimes it will be appropriate for therapeutic work with the youngster to be undertaken by the fieldworker who is not a part of day-to-day living in the unit, and for work with the family to be undertaken by the residential worker, who is likely to be able to empathise with parents as a result of greater knowledge of the particular difficulties of the young person. It will be desirable for one worker to be identified who will be responsible for coordination and accountable for ensuring that either agreements are adhered to, or appropriate changes made. The views of such a worker should not, however, be given any more weight in decisions about ways of helping youngsters that those of the carers, the youngsters themselves, and other important people in their lives, such as parents.

Agreements should include discussions about the recording process; who will have access to records; and what sort of information will be shared with whom. The Children Act guidance and regulations on residential care and leaving care (Volumes 3 and 4) are essential reading for anyone placing a child in residential care.

Social work with the children

There are many excellent books on social work practice with children and young people in residential care, some written by practitioners about their own special way of working, and others seeking common ground in the group care experience. Those which I have found most useful are listed in Appendix 2.

Many of the techniques for working with children which I have already discussed, are appropriate for working with youngsters in residential care, either in groups or individually. Many residential workers and foster parents are becoming skilled in undertaking life-story work, and are in a particularly good position to pick the right moment to do this work. Skills developed by juvenile justice workers are also appropriate, either with individuals or groups.

Stigma is often a particular difficulty for youngsters in residential care. Workers must concern themselves with minimising stigma resulting from institutionalising regimes, and also with helping youngsters to find 'cover stories' and develop coping mechanisms to help alleviate any difficulties resulting from living in a children's home or foster home. For older children, self-help groups will be particularly appropriate. Young people should be routinely offered the literature of the National Association for Young People in Care, and help to form local groups should be made available, but in an unobtrusive way.

Social work with the carers

If this type of placement is to be successful, the care-givers must be full partners in the process of helping the youngster. The main social work role will be identifying those who can take such young people into their homes, and offering training and consultation.

Support groups for specialist foster parents are a major strength of such schemes, and it is important for social workers and managers not to feel threatened if such groups express strong views about the management of the service to adolescents in difficulties. People attracted to this role are often strongly independent – and determined fighters for the interests of the children in their care. It is not unknown for those who fight for their children to be labelled as trouble-makers when they refuse to compromise, or take requests for a particular kind of help to a higher level if it is initially refused. It is this very determination which allows them to persist in offering a home to a youngster despite many set-backs and considerable discomfort to themselves and their families.

Both residential workers and specialist foster parents find the constraints of bureaucracy difficult to cope with. White (1979) described the local authority system as 'thoroughly institutional and institutionalising'; and the Residential Care Association, in its evidence to the Barclay Committee, questioned whether the 'size and structure [of local authorities] will ever permit them to respond flexibly enough to permit residential establishments to fulfil their roles, without a major change of attitudes' (NISW 1982). Potter (1986), in describing her visits to children's homes, notes that

> the point was made time and time again that bureaucracy is in opposition to good residential care. Whether it was the intrusiveness of reviews on children living a normal life within the family of a voluntary children's home; the imposition of staffing requirements and record keeping on a large family registered as a home; or, the project leader of an adolescent unit battling to get decent tea-bags, wallpaper, duvet covers and sag-bags and to find a code in the expenditure for a shed for the goat and food for the cats – the point was the same: the administrative procedures prohibit the provision of a real Home for children in care. (Potter 1986: 29)

It is also important that carers should have a major role in deciding who should live in their foster or residential units. Berridge (1985) describes the impossible task of those residential facilities which are not allowed to have a say about the youngsters for whom the regime they offer is most appropriate, so that they end up with a middle-of-the-road regime which is appropriate to no one.

As with other long-term placements, it is essential for the young people and their parents or present carers to visit the proposed foster home or residential unit, and also for the proposed carers to visit the parents if there is any likelihood of continued contact. If at all possible a choice should be offered to a young person between residential care and specialist foster care, with both placements being visited by the young person and parents so that everyone is in possession of the same information before decisions are taken. If this is to happen, decisions about placement must lie with those principally involved – the youngster, his or her parents, the current care-givers, the potential new care-givers and the social worker. Thus managerial arrangements which rely on panels to allocate beds to bodies are totally inappropriate.

Social work with natural parents

Unless the structures of the care authorities are able to give parents a real sense of involvement in the way in which their children are cared for, the sense of alienation, bewilderment or even betrayal which they feel is likely to intervene and stop them joining with fieldworkers and carers to help their children.

Recognising the damage which the apathy of parents did to youngsters in long-term residential care, Barnardo's Scottish division initiated its family social work project (Massey and Peacey 1983). Field social workers were attached to the long-term residential units and schools, in order to prevent some youngsters drifting into long-term care but also because

> there is little point in placing children with emotional and behavioural problems in costly residential and special education units, if we fail to acknowledge that a child with such difficulties usually belongs to a family experiencing a combination of environmental, health and emotional problems. (Massey and Peacey 1983: 97)

Workers with small caseloads are therefore allocated to families even when there is no likelihood of the youngster returning home, to help them to identify – and feel some confidence in – playing whatever role they can still perform.

> This may be the last opportunity to hold and work with the confusion and chaos, which handicaps both the child and the family. (*Ibid.*)

As with other placements, the style of work appropriate to each family will vary, ranging from welfare rights work and consciousness-raising group work through to person-centred counselling to help build self-esteem. The style of work undertaken with the parents will, to some extent, depend on the plans for the child's future and the methods for achieving these plans. Where therapy is offered in order to facilitate a return home, or mend disrupted relationships, family therapy or family group conferences will often be appropriate, perhaps alongside other methods. Where a young person is to leave local authority accommodation and move on to live independently, social work with the natural parents, which enhances their self-esteem and coping skills, will probably be the most valuable tool in enabling them to play a useful role as their son or daughter moves into adulthood.

Case example 3: James Jones

James is the second son of Bill and Enid Jones. Enid had a psychiatric breakdown in her late teens, leading to in-patient treatment for six months. The diagnosis was unclear, although the labels 'psychotic' and 'schizophrenic' appear on her file.

She married late; Eddy being born when she was 38 and James when she was 40. Her husband, Bill, was a placid and caring husband and father, who cushioned the two boys from her frequent episodes of agitated or depressed behaviour. However, there was concern from relatives and neighbours about whether Enid was too 'heavy-handed' with James, a very active (? hyperactive) youngster, always up to mischief, wandering off from a very early age and destructive with his toys and household possessions. However, her love for and pride in the boys was not in dispute.

When James was eight, Bill died suddenly after a heart attack. Enid was grief-stricken and had to be sedated. James appeared not to be concerned. About a year later the school reported that James had been beaten by his mother with a stick. A child protection conference was called. Enid willingly accepted the offer of counselling for herself (focusing on the loss of her husband and her feelings about being left alone to care for the boys) and James attended a weekly group at the family centre.

Eddy was placid and seemed not to come into conflict with his mother, but it soon became clear that James and Enid were frequently in serious conflict and that at such times both became extremely agitated and fought with each other. Such episodes usually ended in James either barricading himself in his room and systematically destroying the furniture, or running off – often to be brought back by the police late at night.

The risk of him being seriously injured by his mother, who was a powerfully built woman and described by neighbours as often 'out of control', led, after one such episode, to him being taken into police protection and to a care order.

He went first to a children's home for a period of assessment. His mother and Eddy were encouraged to visit, and James also went home for weekends about once a month. However, such visits were fraught with tension. With James's and Enid's agreement it was decided that a long-term foster home should be sought, where contact could be maintained. Psychiatric assessment of Enid and of James turned up nothing of significance, except a personality clash due to James's level of activity and destructiveness and Enid's 'short fuse' and overly high expectations of good behaviour. An attempt to get James to look at his reaction to his father's death was kept firmly at bay by a repertoire of defences.

After careful preparation, James, now aged ten, moved into a long-term foster home. He was keen to go and the family were confident after several weekend visits that he would fit in well. His mother said she liked the family and agreed with the plan for him to visit home for a weekend each month. For almost 12 months there were no difficulties, but he then started to systematically undermine the placement. He destroyed the cherished possessions of the other children in the family; ran home to his mother in the early hours of the morning and had to be forcibly brought back by the police; and, final straw, stood hysterically in the middle of the school playground calling the foster family and their children all the unpleasant names he knew, much to the embarrassment of his foster brother.

Another assessment period in a 'bridge' foster home followed. Both James and his mother were fairly sure that placement back home would not work, but they wanted to stay in touch. In the light of hindsight there seemed to be reasons why the particular circumstances of the first foster family had been the wrong choice. So again after careful preparation, James was placed with another long-term foster family, with the possibility of adoption if all went well. This time he was the youngest child. This placement lasted another 12 months and followed a similar pattern. By this time James was having weekly sessions with a behavioural psychologist, who was also advising the foster parents on how to cope with his destructive outbursts. The outbursts were interspersed with spells of telling 'tall stories' which were too unbelievable to be called lies but which his foster parents found even more difficult to take than his bouts of aggression.

Another 'bridge' foster home, and another 'long-term' foster placement followed, since the 'bridge' foster family, and the family centre where he was placed during the day, could not understand why the last foster family had found him so difficult. This one lasted until he was 14, when it was decided that a residential placement was appropriate. He had some stability in his children's home, although it was not really able to do much about his underlying problems as it was characterised by lots of comings and goings. At 16½ he moved on to a hostel and at 18 moved out of care, still with severe problems in sustaining relationships, but with tenuous contacts with his mother, brother, an aunt, his last foster parents and the staff of the hostel.

With hindsight (and the signs were all there to be read at the time) James should have been placed in a 'family-alternative' placement when his first long-term placement broke down. The legacy of early experiences – which despite many hours of therapy he kept hidden behind a protective screen of constant activity or anger – with professionals and would-be substitute parents alike, would not let him accept another family.

A long-term placement, either with skilled 'professional' foster parents or in a children's home able to provide long-term help and care, could have offered him a place where he could have learned to trust adults and make peace with himself and his past. He might then have been able, perhaps in his mid-teens, to move back to his mother and Eddy, or on to a substitute family (perhaps one of his relatives). Alternatively he might have developed a 'sense of permanence', secure in the knowledge that he was cared about by 'non-parental' adults who would not require him to move on until he was ready for it, and that his mother and Eddy would continue to care about him although he could not live with them.

9 After placement and after care

The model of practice outlined in this book is based on the principles of partnership and of permanence.

As the 1987 White Paper in proposing changes to child care law points out, preparation for a child leaving care 'should be a continuing process throughout the child's time with the local authority'. That means aiming not simply to prevent 'drift'; to place a child for adoption; or to prepare a youngster for independent living (although these are important instrumental aims), but the provision of opportunities to love and be loved, to give and to take from people who really do care. Where we fail in achieving this goal – and it seems that even with highly skilled work on average at least 20 per cent of the 'permanent' placements we make will not work out – then we must go on offering professional support to the youngsters who leave care, carefully exploring with them how best to help as they move into adult relationships and start their own new families.

Partnership with professional colleagues, but above all with the children, their parents, relatives, neighbours and care-givers, is an essential ingredient of a policy which aims to ensure that they have a secure base when they leave our care. It is a truism to say that our major colleagues are our clients. Without their efforts and commitment, all our *professional* efforts will fail, and they will not be committed to our plans unless these plans and the way we put them into operation make sense to them.

Of course, there will be conflicts, and the skills of conciliation and negotiation will then be crucially important. Sometimes conflict will result in the ending of contact between a child and his or her parents. But to make this decision unless it is absolutely necessary, especially if it is against the wishes of the parents or child, is an abuse of our power. We must always remember that for a child to lose parents and siblings is also to lose grandparents, aunts and uncles for that future adult's children. I can think of many parents who have not made too good a job of parenting their own youngsters, but whose support as grandparents has played an important part in helping a next generation family to stay together. I shudder for 'James' as he starts to bring up his own family without the prospect of support from close relatives.

Thus the attempt to work in partnership with parents must continue after placement, even if their child has become attached to and fully accepted by a permanent new family. We should try to ensure that members of the first family have regular news of a youngster's progress, if direct contact with the child and new family is not possible or desirable, and that the child has accurate information about changes occurring within the family of origin. The problems of 'searching', which now figure prominently in the adoption literature, do not become problems if parents, children and siblings do not totally lose contact.

Also, as we have seen, child placement is not an exact science. If we don't get it right, contingency plans involving members of the natural family are not possible if we have totally lost or alienated them. Young people who are still looked after at 18, and are not well settled with a foster family, will need all our skills as negotiators with members of their natural families and peer groups, potential employers or landladies. They will also need the practical and befriending services spelled out in the Children Act guidance on services for young people leaving care or accommodation (Volume 3).

I have stressed throughout the book that placement decisions must start with a careful assessment of each child's needs, and proceed with the creative use of legal provisions, skills in family social work, and the recruitment and support of supplementary or substitute parents in order to meet these needs. A model of practice which stresses the involvement of the children – with the worker carefully listening to what they are saying and observing the signals they are giving – will allow a fuller assessment of their wishes and needs, and of areas where compromises *can* be made and must *not* be made.

Partnership with the carers, whether natural parents, relatives, substitute parents or 'professional' carers, is based on our understanding of their style of caring and parenting. This understanding must be built up at the recruitment and matching stages, so that children are not placed with families whose way of doing things does not allow a particular child's needs to be met. For social workers must accept that no amount of 'back-seat driving' can fundamentally change a family's way of functioning, and that well-meaning but inappropriate advice will merely add to the stresses on children and parents alike. We can use our skills and knowledge to help with temporary problems, and we must be available when needed to offer encouragement, or just a listening ear, but our way of intervening must always make sense to them. It is for this reason that the preceding chapters have not followed the usual format based on legal status, such as adoption or fostering, but have grouped types of placement in terms of what they offer different groups of children and their implications for the nature of the social work service.

The research studies I have referred to have shown that there is no formula which can be neatly applied to a child needing placement. They have shown that child care work is often either unnecessarily rushed, or shows little awareness of the effects of the passage of time on a child's life.

But they have also identified areas of effective practice with children, with their families and with new families, and have suggested that the essential ingredients of such practice are the same whatever placement is chosen. This work cannot be undertaken satisfactorily by those who lack detailed knowledge and skills, who are overstretched by the demands of too large a caseload, who do not have regular time to consult with someone who knows them and their cases well or who are inadequately supervised and feel unsupported in taking necessary risks.

Child placement is a costly enterprise in terms of the emotional energy of all those involved, as well as of finances and professional time. And so it should be. Children are our future, and children at risk of permanent separation from their families need our care and protection. On utilitarian and humanitarian grounds we have to ensure that those – like 'James' – who embark on adult life at 18 with no one close enough to really care about them, or for whom they really care, are as few in number as all our skill and energy can make them.

Appendix 1
Summary of child care law and statistics for Northern Ireland, Scotland and Wales

Northern Ireland

The major child care statutes in Northern Ireland are the Children and Young Persons (N.I.) Act 1968, which covers children on fit person orders as well as those in 'voluntary' care, and the Adoption (N.I.) Order 1987. The Northern Ireland equivalent of Section 1 of the Children Act 1989, is Section 164 of the Children and Young Persons (N.I.) Act 1968. A Children Order (N.I.) is in preparation and it is expected to mirror the provisions in the Children Act 1989.

There were 2876 children in care in Northern Ireland in March 1991. This represents a growth of 14 per cent compared to the total in 1985. Of these, 18 per cent were under school age and 15 per cent were over school-leaving age. In the year to the end of March 1991 there were 1058 admissions to care and 970 discharges. A third of the discharges occurred after less than two months in care and 55 per cent took place within 12 months of admission. There were 1502 children on the Child Protection Register. For the three Area Boards for which figures were available, 16 per cent of these registrations were for actual or suspected sexual abuse.

Scotland

There are important differences between child care law and the legal systems in England and Scotland. (See Macleod, S. and Giltinnan, D. (1987) for a summary of child care law in Scotland. See also the *Review of Child Care Law in Scotland* which discussed options for reform of the law in Scotland.) The Social Work (Scotland) Act 1968 makes provision for voluntary reception into care, and the assumption of parental rights by administrative action. Adoption law is the same as in England and Wales. Help to maintain families in their own homes is governed by the provisions of Section 12 of the Social Work (Scotland) Act 1968. In cases where statutory action is considered appropriate, the Children's Hearings decide whether a supervision requirement is necessary, whether a youngster should be supervised at home or in care, and, in some cases, the nature of parental access. All cases are reviewed annually, and often more frequently, by a hearing. Children subject to parental rights resolutions can be placed at home under supervision.

Because of the different legislative framework the statistics are not strictly comparable. In Scotland 4733 children were in care or under residential supervision in March 1989. There were 7304 children who were the subject of supervision requirements in their own homes. Of those away from home, approximately 37 per cent were in voluntary care; and 63 per cent in statutory care, either through a court order or a parental rights resolution. Seventeen per cent of the 12037 who were in care or under supervision requirements were under five and 56 per cent were aged 12 or over.

In 1988–89, of 3595 children who were admitted to care or residential supervision, 55 per cent came into 'voluntary' care. There were 3095 children who were made the subjects of non-residential supervision orders or other court orders. (For further details see *Statistical Bulletin CC13/1990*, Scottish Education Department, Social Work Services Group 1990.)

Wales

Child care law in England and Wales is the same. There were 3177 children in care in Wales in March 1991. Nearly 17 per cent were under five, and 61 per cent were aged ten or over. Thirty-two per cent were in care 'voluntarily' and 67 per cent under a court order or parental rights resolution.

There were 2 697 'care episodes' in 1990–91. Half involved children aged ten or over, and half involved children under five. Half came into care voluntarily and half left home under a care or other court order. (For further details see *Children in Care or under Supervision Orders in Wales: Year ended 31.3.85*, Welsh Office 1986.)

Appendix 2
Selected reading for child care practitioners

Chapters 1 and 2

An overview of child placement and the children who may need it

Berridge and Cleaver 1987	Packman *et al.* 1986
Blackburn 1991	Parker 1990
DH 1991c	Parker *et al.* 1991
Gibbons *et al.* 1990	Rowe *et al.* 1989
Millham *et al.* 1986	

Chapter 3

On general principles and the law

Ball 1991	Freeman 1992
DH 1989a, 1989b, 1991a	Newell 1991
Fox-Harding 1991	

On social work with families

Ahmed *et al.* 1986	Holman 1988
Aldgate 1989	Howe 1987
Aldgate and Bradley 1993	Macdonald 1991
Family Rights Group 1991	Maluccio *et al.* 1986
Gibbons 1992	Moore 1992
Gibbons *et al.* 1990	
Hardiker *et al.* 1991	Stevenson 1989

On social work with children

Aldgate and Simmonds 1987
Aldgate *et al.* 1989
Batty 1991
Bee 1989
Fahlberg 1988
Jones 1992

Redgrave 1987
Ryan and Walker 1985
Stein and Carey 1986
Wilson *et al.* 1992
Winnicott 1986

Chapter 4

Choice of placement

BAAF 1991
Bryer 1988
Cliffe and Berridge 1991
DH 1989b

Maluccio *et al.* 1986
Parker 1980
Parker *et al.* 1991
Thoburn 1990

Chapter 5

Restoration to natural parents

Aldgate 1989
Bullock *et al.* 1993
Dartington 1992
Family Rights Group 1986, 1992
Farmer and Parker 1991
Gibbons 1992

Lewis *et al.* 1992
Marsh and Triseliotis 1993
Mattinson and Sinclair 1979
Moore 1992
Thoburn 1980
Trent 1989

Chapter 6

On placement with relations

Berridge and Cleaver 1987
Bullard *et al.* 1990
Dartington 1992
De'Ath 1992
DH 1992

Farmer and Parker 1991
Masson *et al.* 1983
Rowe *et al.* 1984
Trent 1989

Chapter 7

On placement with substitute parents
Aldgate *et al.* 1989
Argent 1988
Batty 1991
Fahlberg 1988
Fitzgerald 1983
Fitzgerald *et al.* 1982
Fratter *et al.* 1991
Hill *et al.* 1989

Howe 1992
Jewett 1984
Macaskill 1985
Mullender 1991
Thoburn 1990
Thoburn *et al.* 1986
Triseliotis 1988
Wedge and Mantle 1991

Chapter 8

On placement in group care
Atherton 1989
Berridge 1985
Collins and Bruce 1984
Davis 1981
Fahlberg 1990
Hazel 1981
Lennox 1982

Potter 1986
Rose 1990
Shaw and Hipgrave 1983
Social Services Inspectorate
   1991
Stein and Carey 1986

Bibliography

Adcock, M., White, R. and Hollows, A. (1991), *Significant Harm*, Croydon: Significant Publications.

Ahmed, S., Cheetham, J. and Small, J. (1986), *Social Work with Black Children and their Families*, London: Batsford/BAAF.

Aldgate, J. (1980), 'Identification of Factors which Influence Length of Stay in Care', in J. P. Triseliotis (ed.), *New Developments in Foster Care and Adoption*, London: Routledge and Kegan Paul.

Aldgate, J. (ed.), (1989), *Using Written Agreements with Children and Families*, London: Family Rights Group.

Aldgate, J. and Bradley, M. (1993), *A Guide to the Provision of Respite Care*, London: HMSO.

Aldgate, J., Maluccio, A. N. and Reeves, C. (1989), *Adolescents in Foster Families*, London : Batsford.

Aldgate, J. and Simmonds, J. (eds), (1987), *Direct Work with Children*, London: Batsford/BAAF.

Argent, H. (ed.), (1988), *Keeping the Doors Open*, London: BAAF.

Atherton, C. (1986), 'The Importance and Purpose of Access' and 'The Family's Experiences of Difficulties in Access' in C. Atherton (ed.), *Promoting Links: Keeping Children and Families in Touch*, London: FRG.

Atherton, J. (1989), *Interpreting Residential Life: Values to Practice*, London: Routledge.

Balbernie, R. (1972), *Residential Work with Children*, London: Pergamon.

Ball, C. (1991), *Social Work Law File: Child Care Law*, Norwich: UEA Monographs.

Ball, C. (1992), *Law for Social Workers: An Introduction*, Aldershot: Ashgate.

Banks, N. (1992), 'Techniques for Direct Identity Work with Black Children', *Adoption and Fostering*, 16, (3).

Banks, S. and Grizell, R. (1984), *A Study of Specialist Fostering in Essex*, London: Social Services Inspectorate.

Barnado's Yorkshire Division (1986), *New Families in Yorkshire*, Bradford: Barnardo's, 47 Darley Street.

Barry, P. (1987), 'Community Provision for Children in Trouble: the South Glamorgan Experience', MSW dissertation, Norwich: University of East Anglia.

Batty, D. (ed.), (1991), *Sexually Abused Children: Making their Placements Work*, London: BAAF.

Batty, D. (ed.), (1993), *HIV Infection and Children in Need*, London: BAAF.

Bebbington, A. and Miles, J. (1989), 'The Background of Children who Enter Local Authority Care,' *British Journal of Social Work*, **15**, (5).

Becker, S. and MacPherson, S. (eds), (1988), *Public Issues, Private Pain*, London: Social Services Insight.

Bee, H. (1989), *The Developing Child*, New York: Harper and Row.

Berridge, D. (1985), *Children's Homes*, Oxford: Blackwell.

Berridge, D. and Cleaver, H. (1987), *Foster Home Breakdown*, Oxford: Basil Blackwell.

Bettelheim, B. (1955), *Truants from Life*, New York: The Free Press.

Blackburn, C. (1991), *Poverty and Health: Working with Families*, Milton Keynes: Open University.

Bowlby, J. (1971), *Attachment and Loss*, London: Penguin.

Bowlby, J. (1979), *The Making and Breaking of Affectional Bonds*, London: Tavistock.

Bowlby, J. (1988), *A Secure Base*, London: Tavistock/Routledge.

British Agencies for Adoption and Fostering (1986), *Working with Children*, London: BAAF.

British Agencies for Adoption and Fostering (1991), 'Managing Statutory Reviews', Training pack, London: BAAF.

British Association of Social Workers (1980), *Clients are Fellow Citizens*, Birmingham: BASW.

British Association of Social Workers (1982), *Guidelines for Practice in Family Placement*, Birmingham: BASW.

British Association of Social Workers (1987), *Code of Practice on Prevention and Rehabilitation*, Birmingham: BASW.

Brown, D. (1982), *The Step-Family: A Growing Challenge for Social Work*, Norwich: SWT/UEA Monographs.

Brown, G. and Harris, T. (1978), *The Social Origins of Depression: A Study of Psychiatric Disorders in Women*, London: Tavistock.

Bryer, M. (1988), *Planning in Child Care*, London: BAAF.

Bullard, E. and Malos, E. with Parker, R. (1990), 'Custodianship, A Report to the Department of Health', Bristol: University of Bristol.

Bullock, R., Little, M. and Millham, S. (1993), *Going Home*, Aldershot: Dartmouth.

Burch, M. (1986), 'Shared Care and Responsibility: A Foster Parent's View', in *Promoting Links: Keeping Children and Families in Touch*, London: Family Rights Group.

Burgoyne, J. and Clark, D. (1982), 'Reconstituted Families' in R. N. Rapoport, M. P. Fogarty and R. Rapoport (eds), *Families in Britain*, London: Routledge and Kegan Paul.

Caesar, G., Parchment, M., Berridge, D. and Gordon, G. (1993), *Black Perspectives on Services for Children and Young People in Need and Their Families*, London: National Children's Bureau/Barnardo's.

Cairns, B. (1984), 'The Children's Family Trust: a Unique Approach to Substitute Family Care?', *British Journal of Social Work*, **14**, 457–473.

Charles, M., Rashid, S. P. and Thoburn, J. (1992), 'The Placement of Black Children with Permanent New Families', *Adoption and Fostering*, **16**, (3).

Children's Legal Centre and Department of Health (1992), *Living Away from Home: Your Rights*, London: HMSO.

Cliffe, D. and Berridge, D. (1991), *Closing Children's Homes*, London: National Children's Bureau.

Collins, T. and Bruce, T. (1984), *Staff Support and Staff Training*, London: Tavistock.

Colton, M. (1989), *Dimensions of Substitute Care*, Aldershot: Avebury.

Cooper, J. (1978), *Patterns of Family Placement*, London: National Children's Bureau.

Cox, A., Pound, A. and Puckering, C. (1992), 'NEWPIN: A Befriending Scheme and Therapeutic Network for Carers of Young Children' in J. Gibbons (ed.), *The Children Act 1989 and Family Support*, London: HMSO.

Dartington Social Research Unit (1992), *Going Home: Key Factors in the Return Process*, Dartington: Social Research Unit.

Davis, A. (1981), *The Residential Solution*, London: Tavistock.

De'Ath, E. (ed.), (1992), *Stepfamilies: What do we Know? What do we Need to Know?*, Croydon: Significant Publications.

Department of Health and Social Security (1972), *Report of the Departmental Committee on the Adoption of Children*, (Houghton Report), London: HMSO.

Department of Health and Social Security (1974), *Report of the Committee of Inquiry into the Care and Supervision Provided in Relation to Maria Colwell*, London: HMSO.

Department of Health and Social Security (1976), *Foster Care: A Guide to Practice*, London: HMSO.

Department of Health and Social Security (1983), *Code of Practice on Access to Children in Care*, London: HMSO.

Department of Health and Social Security (1984a), *A Study of Specialist Fostering in Essex*, London: Social Work Service.

Department of Health and Social Security (1984b), *Adoption Agencies Regulations, 1983, Local Authority Circular LAC (1984)* **3**, London: DHSS.

Department of Health and Social Security (1985), *Social Work Decisions in Child Care: Recent Research Findings and their Implications*, London: HMSO.

Department of Health and Social Security (1987), *The Law on Child Care and Family Services*, London: HMSO.

Department of Health and Social Security (1988), *Protecting children: A Guide for Social Workers Undertaking a Comprehensive Assessment*,

London: HMSO.
Department of Health (1989a), *An Introduction to the Children Act, 1989*, London: HMSO.
Department of Health (1989b), *Principles and Practice in Regulations and Guidance*, London: HMSO.
Department of Health (1991a), *The Children Act Guides for Parents, Children and Young People*, London: DH.
Department of Health (1991b), *The Children Act, 1989, Guidance and Regulations*, **1–10**, London: HMSO.
Department of Health (1991c), *Patterns and Outcomes in Child Placement*, London: HMSO.
Department of Health (1991d), *Working Together under the Children Act 1989*, London: HMSO.
Department of Health (1992), *Review of Adoption Law: A Consultation Document*, London: HMSO.
Department of Health (1993), *Children Act Report, 1992*, London: HMSO.
Docker-Drysdale, B. (1968), *Therapy in Child Care*, London: Longmans.
Doel, M. and Marsh, P. (1992), *Task-centred Social Work*, Aldershot: Ashgate.
Dominelli, L. (1988), *Anti-racist Social Work*, London: Macmillan.
Donley, K. (1975), *Opening New Doors*, London: BAAF.
Donnelly, A. (1986), *Feminist Social Work with a Women's Group*, Norwich: SWT/UEA Social Work Monographs.
Dyde, W. (1987), *Place of Safety Orders*, Norwich: SWT/UEA Social Work Monographs.
England, H. (1986), *Social Work as Art: Making Sense of Good Practice*, London: Allen and Unwin.
Erikson, E. H. (1965), *Identity, Youth and Crisis*, London: Hogarth Press.
Erikson, E. H. (1983), *Childhood and Society*, London: Hogarth Press.
Essen, J. and Wedge, P. (1982), *Continuities in Childhood Disadvantage*, London: Heinemann.
Fahlberg, V. (1988), *Fitting the Pieces Together*, London: BAAF.
Fahlberg, V. (1990), *Residential Treatment: A Tapestry of many Therapies*, New York: Perspectives Press.
Family Rights Group (1982), *Fostering Parental Contact*, London: FRG.
Family Rights Group (1985), *The Link Between Prevention and Care*, London: FRG.
Family Rights Group (1986), *Promoting Links: Keeping Children and Families in Touch*, London: FRG.
Family Rights Group (1991), *The Children Act, 1989: Working in Partnership with Families*, London: FRG.
Family Rights Group/National Foster Care Association (1991), *Children Act 1989 Written Agreement Forms*, London: FRG/NFCA.
Family Rights Group and NSPCC (1992), *Child Protection Procedures: What They Mean for Your Family*, London: FRG/NSPCC.
Fanshel, D. and Shinn, E. B. (1978), *Children in Foster Care – A Longitudinal Study*, New York: Columbia University Press.
Farmer, E. and Parker, R. A. (1985), *A Study of the Discharge of Care*

Orders, Bristol: University of Bristol, School of Applied Social Studies.

Farmer, E. and Parker, R. A. (1991), *Trials and Tribulations*, London: HMSO.

Fein, E., Maluccio, A. N., Hamilton, V. J. and Ward, D. E. (1983), 'After Foster Care: Permanency Planning for Children', *Child Welfare*, **62**, (6), 485–567.

Finkelhor, D. (1986), *A Sourcebook on Child Sexual Abuse*, New York: Sage.

Fisher, M., Marsh, P. and Phillips, D. with Sainsbury, E. (1986), *In and Out of Care: The Experiences of Children, Parents and Social Workers*, London: Batsford/BAAF.

Fitzgerald, J. (1983), *Understanding Disruption*, London: BAAF.

Fitzgerald, J., Murcer, B. and Murcer, B. (1982), *Building New Families Through Adoption and Fostering*, Oxford: Blackwell.

Ford, J. (1983), *Human Behaviour: Towards a Practical Understanding*, London: Routledge and Kegan Paul.

Fox-Harding, L. (1991), *Perspectives in Child Care Policy*, London: Longman.

Fratter, J., Newton, D. and Shinegold, D. (1982), *Cambridge Cottage Pre-Fostering and Adoption Unit*, Barkingside, Essex: Barnardo Social Work Papers, No. 16.

Fratter, J., Rowe, J., Sapsford, D. and Thoburn, J. (1991), *Permanent Family Placement: A Decade of Experience*, London: BAAF.

Freeman, I. and Montgomery, S. (eds), (1988), *Child Care: Monitoring Practice*, London: Jessica Kingsley.

Freeman, M. D. A. (1992), *Children, their Families and the Law*, Basingstoke: Macmillan.

Fuller, R. and Stevenson, O. (1983), *Policies, Programmes and Disadvantage*, London: Heinemann.

Gibbons, J. with Thorpe, S. and Wilkinson, P. (1990), *Family Support and Prevention*, London: HMSO.

Gibbons, J. (ed.), (1992), *The Children Act, 1989 and Family Support: Principles into Practice*, London: HMSO.

Gill, O. and Jackson, B. (1982), *Adoption and Race*, London: Batsford.

Hardiker, P., Exton, K. and Barker, M. (1991), *Policies and Practices in Preventive Child Care*, Aldershot: Avebury.

Harlow Parents' Aid (1991), *Guide for Parents with Children in Care*, Parents' Aid, 66 Chippingfield, Harlow.

Hazel, N. (1981), *A Bridge to Independence*, Oxford: Blackwell.

Hill, M., Lambert, L. and Triseliotis, J. (1989), *Achieving Adoption with Love and Money*, London: National Children's Bureau.

Hoggan, P. and O'Hara, G. (1988), 'Permanent Substitute Family Care in Lothian – Placement Outcome', *Adoption and Fostering*, **12**, (3).

Hoghughi, M. (1978), *Troubled and Troublesome*, London: Andre Deutsch.

Holman, B. (1976), *Inequality in Child Care*, London: Child Poverty Action Group.

Holman, B. (1978), *Poverty: Explanations of Social Deprivation*, London:

Martin Robertson.

Holman, B. (1981), *Kids at the Door*, Oxford: Basil Blackwell.

Holman, B. (1988), *Putting Families First: Prevention and Child Care*, London: Macmillan.

House of Commons Social Services Committee (1984), *Children in Care*, London: HMSO.

Howe, D. (1986), *Social Workers and their Practice in Welfare Bureaucracies*, Aldershot: Gower.

Howe, D. (1987), *An Introduction to Social Work Theory*, Aldershot: Gower.

Howe, D. (1989), *The Consumers' View of Family Therapy*, Aldershot: Gower.

Howe, D. (1992), 'Assessing Adoptions in Difficulty', *British Journal of Social Work*, **22**, (1).

Jenkins, S. and Norman, E. (1972), *Filial Deprivation and Foster Care*, New York: Columbia University Press.

Jewett, C. (1984), *Helping Children Cope with Separation and Loss*, London: Batsford/BAAF.

Jones, D. (1987), *Understanding Child Abuse*, London: Macmillan.

Jones, D. P. H. (1992), *Interviewing the Sexually Abused Child*, 4th edn, London: Gaskell/Royal College of Physicians.

Jones, M. A. (1985), *A Second Chance for Families: Five Years Later: Follow-up of a Programme to Prevent Foster Care*, New York: Child Welfare League of America.

Jones, M. A. , Neuman, R. and Shyne, A. W. (1976), *A Second Chance for Families: Evaluation of a Programme to Reduce Foster Care*, New York: Child Welfare League of America.

Jordan, B. (1973), *Poor Parents*, London: Routledge and Kegan Paul.

Jordan, B. (1979), *Helping in Social Work*, London: Routledge and Kegan Paul.

Jordan, B. (1990), *Social Work in an Unjust Society*, London: Harvester Wheatsheaf.

Kadushin, A. (1970), *Adopting Older Children*, New York: Columbia University Press.

Kelly, G. (1990), *Patterns of Care*, Belfast: Queens University.

Kennedy, M. and Kelly, L. (eds), (1992), *Child Abuse Review*: Special issue on abuse and children with disabilities, **1**, (3).

King, M. and Trowell, J. (1992), *Children's Welfare and the Law*, London: Sage.

Lahti, J. (1982), 'A Follow-up Study of Foster Children in Permanent Placements', *Social Service Review*, University of Chicago, 556–571.

Lambert, L. and Streather, J. (1980), *Children in Changing Families*, London: Macmillan.

Lennox, D. (1982), *Residential Group Therapy for Children*, London: Tavistock.

Leonard, P. (1984), *Personality and Ideology: Towards a Materialist Understanding of the Individual*, London: Macmillan.

Lewis, A., Shemmings, D. and Thoburn, J. (1992), 'Participation in

Practice Involving Families in Child Protection' (Training pack), Norwich: UEA.

Liddy, J. (1970), 'The Self-image of the Child Placed with Relatives', *Smith College Studies in Social Work*, **40**, (2).

Liffman, M. (1978), *Power for the Poor*, Sydney: Allen and Unwin.

London Borough of Brent (1985), 'A Child in Trust. The Report of the Panel of Inquiry into the Circumstances surrounding the Death of Jasmine Beckford', London: Brent Social Services Department.

London Borough of Lambeth (1987), 'The Report of the Panel appointed to inquire into the Death of Tyra Henry', London: Lambeth.

Lowe, J. (1987), *Social Work and Angry Parents*, Norwich: SWT/UEA Monographs.

Lowe, N. (1991), 'The Legal Position of Grandparents under the Children Act 1989' in *What's in it for Grandparents*, Harlow: Grandparents' Federation.

Lynch, M. and Roberts, J. (1982), *Consequences of Child Abuse*, London: Academic Press.

Macaskill, C. (1985), *Against the Odds: Adopting Mentally Handicapped Children*, London: BAAF.

Macaskill, C. (1991), *Adopting or Fostering a Sexually Abused Child*, London: BAAF.

Macdonald, S. (1991), *All Equal Under the Act*, London: Race Equality Unit.

McDonnell, P. and Aldgate, J. (1984), *Reviews of Children in Care*, Oxford: Barnett House Papers.

McLeod, E. and Dominelli, L. (1982), 'The Personal and Political: Feminism and Moving Beyond the Integrated Methods Approach', in R. Bailey and P. Lee (eds), *Theory and Practice in Social Work*, Oxford: Basil Blackwell.

Macleod, S. and Giltinnan, D. (1987), *Child Care Law in Scotland*, London: BAAF.

Madge, N. (ed.), (1983), *Families at Risk*, London: Heinemann.

Maluccio, A. N., Fein, E. and Olmstead, K. A. (1986), *Permanency Planning for Children: Concepts and Methods*, London: Tavistock.

Mann, P. (1984), *Children in Care Revisited*, London: Batsford.

Marsh, P. (1986), 'Natural Families and Children in Care: an Agenda for Practice Development', *Adoption and Fostering*, **10**, (4), 20–25.

Marsh, P. (1991), 'Social Work with Fathers' in Family Rights Group training pack, *The Children Act 1989: Working in Partnership with Families*, London: HMSO.

Marsh, P. and Fisher, M. (1992), *Good Intentions: Developing User-oriented Services under the Children and Community Care Acts*, York: Rowntree.

Marsh, P. and Triseliotis, J. (eds), (1993), *Prevention and Rehabilitation*, London: Batsford.

Massey, S. and Peacey, M. (1983), *Social Work with Families of Children Away from Home*, Barkingside: Barnardo's.

Masson, J., Norbury, D. and Chatterton, S. (1983), *Mine, Yours or Ours?*

A Study of Step-parent Adoption, London, HMSO.

Mattinson, J. and Sinclair, I. (1979), *Mate and Stalemate*, Oxford: Basil Blackwell.

Maximé, J. (1986), 'Some psychological models of black self-concept' in S. Ahmed, J. Cheetham and J. Small (eds), *Social Work with Black Children and their Families*, London: Batsford/BAAF

Miller, J. and Cook, T., (eds), (1981), *Direct Work with Families*, London: Bedford Square Press.

Millham, S., Bullock, R., Hosie, K. and Haak, M. (1986), *Lost in Care: The Problems of Maintaining Links between Children in Care and their Families*, Aldershot: Gower.

Millham, S., Bullock, R., Hosie, K. and Little, M. (1989), *Access Disputes in Child Care*, Aldershot: Gower.

Minuchin, S. (1974), *Families and Family Theapy*, London: Tavistock.

Monaco, M. and Thoburn, J. (1987), *Self-help for Parents with Children in Care*, Norwich: SWT/UEA Social Work Monographs.

Moore, J. (1986), *The ABC of Child Abuse Work*, Aldershot: Gower.

Moore, J. (1992), *The ABC of Child Protection*, Aldershot: Ashgate.

Morris, C. (1984), *The Permanency Principle in Child Care Social Work*, Norwich: SWT/UEA Social Work Monographs.

Mullender, A. (ed.), (1991), *Open Adoption*, London: BAAF.

National Institute for Social Work (1982), 'Social Workers: Their Role and Tasks', Barclay Committee Report, London: Bedford Square Press.

Natural Children's Support Group (1991), *Children Who Foster: Questions and Answers for Children who Foster*, London; BAAF, (video).

Nelson, K. A. (1985), *On the Frontier of Adoption: a Study of Special-needs Adoptive Families*, Washington: Child Welfare League of America.

Newell, P. (1991), *The UN Convention and Children's Rights in the UK*, London: National Children's Bureau.

O'Hara, G. (1986), 'Developing Post-placement Services in Lothian', *Adoption and Fostering*, **10**, (4), 38–42.

Øvretveit, J. (1986), *Improving Social Work Records and Practice*, Birmingham: BASW.

Packman, J. (1981), *The Child's Generation*, 2nd edn, Oxford: Blackwell.

Packman, J. with Randall, J. and Jacques, N. (1986), *Who Needs Care? Social Work Decisions about Children*, Oxford: Basil Blackwell.

Parker, R. A. (1980), *Caring for Separated Children*, London: Macmillan.

Parker, R. A. (1985), 'Planning into practice', *Adoption and Fostering*, **9**, (4), 25–28.

Parker, R. A. (1990), *Away From Home: A History of Child Care*, London: Barnardo's.

Parker, R. A., Ward, H., Jackson, S., Aldgate, J. and Wedge, P. (1991), *Assessing Outcomes in Child Care*, London: HMSO.

Parkinson, L. (1986), *Conciliation in Separation and Divorce*, London: Croom Helm.

Parton, N. (1981), *The Politics of Child Abuse*, Basingstoke: Macmillan.

Parton, N. (1991), *Governing the Family, Child Care, Child Protection and the State*, London: Macmillan.

Pitman, E. (1984), *Transactional Analysis for Social Workers and Counsellors: An Introduction*, London: Routledge and Kegan Paul.

Potter, P. (1986), *Long-Term Residential Care: The Positive Approach*, Norwich: SWT/UEA Social Work Monographs.

Prosser, J. (1992), *Child Abuse Investigations: The Families' Perspectives. A consumer study of 30 families who claim to be falsely accused*, Stanstead: Parents Against Injustice.

Rapoport, R. N., Fogarty, M. P. and Rapoport, R. (eds), (1982), *Families in Britain*, London: Routledge and Kegan Paul.

Raynor, L. (1980), *The Adopted Child Comes of Age*, London: Allen and Unwin.

Redgrave, K. (1987), *Child's Play: Direct Work with the Deprived Child*, Cheadle: Boys and Girls Welfare Society.

Rees, S. (1991), *Achieving Power: Practice and Policy in Social Welfare*, Sydney: Allen and Unwin.

Robinson, M. (1991), *Family Transformation through Divorce and Re-marriage*, London: Routledge.

Rose, M. (1990), *Healing Hurt Minds: The Peper Harrow Experience*, London: Tavistock/Routledge.

Rowe, J., Cain, H., Hundleby, M. and Keane, A. (1984), *Long-Term Foster Care*, London: Batsford.

Rowe, J., Hundleby, M. and Garnett, L. (1989), *Child Care Now*, London: BAAF.

Rushton, A., Treseder, J. and Quinton, D. (1988), *New Parents for Older Children*, London: BAAF.

Rutter, M., Quinton, D. and Liddle, C. (1983), 'Parenting in Two Generations', in N. Madge (ed.), *Families at Risk*, London: Heinemann.

Ryan, T. and Walker, R. (1985), *Life Story Books*, London: BAAF.

Ryburn, M. (1992), video, *Adoption in the 1990s: Identity and Openness*, Leamington: Leamington Press.

Sawbridge, P. (1983), 'Parents for Children', Twelve Practice Papers, London: BAAF.

Scottish Office (1992), *Review of Child Care Law in Scotland*, Edinburgh: HMSO.

Sellick, C. (1992), *Supporting Short-Term Foster Carers*, Aldershot: Avebury.

Shaw, M. and Hipgrave, T. (1983), *Specialist Fostering*, London: Batsford.

Shemmings, D. (1991), *Client Access to Records: Participation in Social Work*, Aldershot, Avebury.

Sinclair, R. (1984), *Decision Making in Statutory Reviews on Children in Care*, Aldershot: Gower.

Small, J. (1986), 'Transracial Placements: Conflicts and Contradictions', in Ahmed, S. *et al.* (eds), *op. cit.*

Smith, T. (1992), 'Family Centres, Children in Need and the Children Act 1989' in J. Gibbons (ed.), *The Children Act 1989 and Family Support*, London: HMSO.

Social Services Inspectorate (1986), *Inspection of the Supervision of Social Workers in the Assessment and Monitoring of Cases of Child Abuse*, London: HMSO.

Social Services Inspectorate (1991), 'Children in the Public Care', Utting Report, London: HMSO.

Stein, M. and Carey, K. (1986), *Leaving Care*, Oxford: Basil Blackwell.

Stein, T. J., Gambrill, E. D. and Wiltse, K. T. (1978), *Children in Foster Homes: Achieving Continuity of Care*, New York: Praeger.

Stevenson, O. (1968), 'Reception into Care: its Meaning for all Concerned', in R. J. N. Tod (ed.), *Children in Care*, London: Longman.

Stevenson, O. (ed.), (1989), *Child Abuse: Public Policy and Professional Practice*, London: Harvester Wheatsheaf.

Stevenson, O. and Smith, J. (1983), 'Report of the Implementation of Section 56 of the Children Act, 1975', Keele: University of Keele, Department of Social Policy and Social Work.

Thoburn, J. (1980), *Captive Clients*, London: Routledge and Kegan Paul.

Thoburn, J. (1986), 'Quality control in Child Care', *British Journal of Social Work*, **16**, 543–566.

Thoburn, J. (1990), *Success and Failure in Permanent Family Placement*, Aldershot: Avebury.

Thoburn, J. (1991a), 'The Children Act 1989; Balancing Child Welfare with the Concept of Partnership with Parents', *Journal of Social Welfare and Family Law*, (1991), (5).

Thoburn, J. (1991b), 'Permanent Family Placement and the Children Act 1989: Implications for Foster Carers and Social Workers', *Adoption and Fostering*, **15**, (3).

Thoburn, J. (1992a), 'A Review of Research which is Relevant to Adoption' in *Review of Adoption Law, a consultation document*, London: HMSO.

Thoburn, J. (ed.), (1992b), *Participation in Practice: A Reader*, Norwich: University of East Anglia.

Thoburn, J., Murdoch, A. and O'Brien, A. (1986), *Permanence in Child Care*, Oxford: Basil Blackwell.

Thoburn, J. and Lewis, A. (1992), 'Partnership with parents of children in need of protection' in J. Gibbons (ed.), *The Children Act 1989 and Family Support*, London: HMSO.

Trent, J. (1989), *Homeward Bound*, London: Barnardo's.

Triseliotis, J. P. (ed.), (1980), *New Developments in Foster Care and Adoption*, London: Routledge and Kegan Paul.

Triseliotis, J. (ed.), (1988), *Groupwork in Adoption and Foster Care*, London: Batsford.

Triseliotis, J. P. and Russell, J. (1984), *Hard to Place – The Outcome of Adoption and Residential Care*, Aldershot: Gower.

Van der Eyken (1982), *Home-start*, Leicester: Home Start Consultancy.

Vernon, J. and Fruin, D. (1986), *In Care: A Study of Social Work Decision Making*, London: National Children's Bureau.

Wedge, P. and Thoburn, J. (eds), (1986), *Finding Families for 'Hard-to-*

place' *Children: Evidence from Research*, London: BAAF.

Wedge, P. and Mantle, G. (1991), *Sibling Groups and Social Work*, Aldershot: Avebury.

Weise, J. (1987), *Trans-racial Adoption: A Black Perspective*, Norwich: SWT/UEA Monographs.

Westacott, J. (1988), *A Bridge to Calmer Waters*, London: Barnardo's.

White, K. (1979), 'United Kingdom Independent Long-stay Children's Homes', in C. Payne and K. White, *Caring for Troubled Children*, London: Croom Helm.

Whittaker, J. K., Kinney, J., Tracy, E. M. and Booth, C. (eds), (1990), *Reaching High Risk Families: Intensive Family Preservation Services*, New York: Aldine de Gruyter.

Wilson, K., Kendrick, P. and Ryan, U. (1992), *Play Therapy: A Non-directive Approach for Children and Adolescents*, London: Ballière Tindall.

Winnicott, C. (1970), *Child Care and Social Work*, Bristol: Bookstall Publications.

Winnicott, C. (1986), 'Face to Face with Children', in *Working with Children*, London: BAAF.

Winnicott, D. W. (1965), *The Family and Individual Development*, London: Tavistock.

Yelloly, M. (1979), *Independent Evaluation of Twenty-five Placements*, Maidstone: Kent County Council.

Index